Costa Rica

Costa Rica

BY NEL YOMTOV

Enchantment of the World™
Second Series

CHILDREN'S PRESS®

An Imprint of Scholastic Inc.

New York   Toronto   London   Auckland   Sydney
Mexico City   New Delhi   Hong Kong
Danbury, Connecticut

Frontispiece: **Costa Rican girl**

Consultant: Oscar Chamosa, Associate Professor of History, University of Georgia, Athens, Georgia

Please note: All statistics are as up-to-date as possible at the time of publication.

Book production by The Design Lab

Library of Congress Cataloging-in-Publication Data
Yomtov, Nelson.
 Costa Rica / by Nel Yomtov.
 pages cm. — (Enchantment of the world, second series)
 Includes bibliographical references and index.
 ISBN 978-0-531-22014-6 (lib. bdg.)
 1. Costa Rica—Juvenile literature. I. Title.
 F1543.2.Y65 2914
 972.86—dc23   2013022563

Red-eyed tree frog

Contents

Left to right: **Costa Rican girl, Lake Arenal, harvesting bananas, zipline, nineteenth-century banana industry**

CHAPTER 1

Welcome to Costa Rica

OR MUCH OF ITS HISTORY, COSTA RICA WAS OFTEN overlooked by the rest of the world. After it was settled by Spain in the 1500s, Costa Rica was a remote colonial outpost. Although Costa Rica means "the rich coast," it had no gold or silver to enrich Spain. As a result, it was nearly ignored by its conquerors. Costa Rica became independent in the 1800s, after three hundred years of colonialism. By the mid-1900s, its policies were gaining attention around the world.

Suffering through a brief civil war in 1948, Costa Rica set out on a path of peace and social reform. While much of Central America was torn apart by violence and war, oppressive military dictatorships, and human rights abuses, Costa Rica flourished as a democracy. Government reforms improved education, health, economic development, and public welfare. The Costa Rican government has remained stable, bolstered by a fair and honest electoral process. Somehow, the tiny nation has managed to avoid the violence and military conflicts that often nip at its borders.

Opposite: **Murals brighten many buildings in San José, the capital of Costa Rica.**

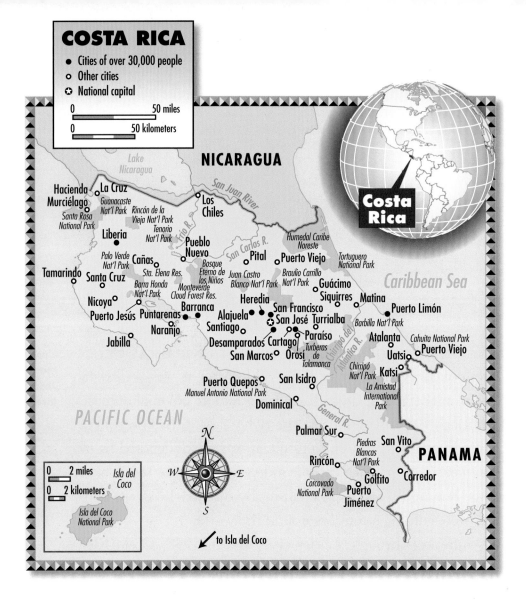

Peace is a top priority to Costa Ricans. The nation's army was abolished in 1948, following the civil war. In 1987, former president Óscar Arias Sánchez was awarded the Nobel Peace Prize for his efforts to end a war in Central America. Today, Costa Rica is home to many large international companies and groups that are attracted by the stability of the nation and friendliness of its people.

In Costa Rica, it is customary for people to have two last names. The first of these last names comes from the person's father and the second from the person's mother. For example, former president Óscar Arias Sánchez is the son of Juan Arias Trejos and Lilliam Sánchez Cortés. Some people use both last names; others drop the second one. The former president is often referred to as Óscar Arias, and his name is alphabetized under A, not S. Costa Rican women do not typically change their names when they marry.

Costa Ricans are proud of their nation's natural beauty and ecological diversity. Towering mountain ranges, lush rain forests, sprawling banana and coffee plantations, peaceful beaches, and active volcanoes dot the landscape. Costa

A Nobel Peace Prize official congratulates Óscar Arias Sánchez (left) after awarding him the prize in 1987.

Rica's mild climate supports an incredible variety of plant and animal life. Thousands of species of plants, trees, birds, butterflies, and other creatures make Costa Rica their home.

In the mid-twentieth century, Costa Rica's population began to increase rapidly. To feed the growing nation, the country's rain forests were cleared to make room for farms and cattle ranches. Hundreds of plant and animal species were endangered, soil erosion increased at an alarming rate, and the nation's waterways became polluted.

To protect its rapidly disappearing natural environment, the government established an extensive system of national parks and nature reserves. Today the country has twenty-eight

About 2,500 different species of plants grow in the Monteverde Cloud Forest Reserve, high in the mountains of Costa Rica.

national parks. Costa Rica has the world's highest percentage of area—more than 25 percent—protected by law.

Costa Rica's trailblazing conservation efforts make it the envy of nations around the world. Although many of the laws are difficult to enforce and environmental problems remain, the country's air and water are getting cleaner. Many nations have consulted with Costa Rica's environmental leaders to learn about their successful programs. Conservation is vital to the nation's economy: Ecotourism, people visiting a place to enjoy its natural beauty, is a booming industry and one that brings in more than a billion dollars in revenues.

Costa Ricans are proud of their peaceful, democratic traditions and commitment to protecting the environment. Warm and friendly, hopeful and optimistic, Costa Ricans look to the future with confidence, eager to tackle the challenges of the twenty-first century.

A tourist enjoys the thrill of riding a zipline through a dense Costa Rican forest.

CHAPTER 2

"The Rich Coast"

COSTA RICA LIES ON THE ISTHMUS OF CENTRAL America, a narrow strip of land that connects the continents of North and South America. Nicaragua lies to the north and Panama to the southeast. Eastern Costa Rica is bordered by the Caribbean Sea, and the western coast lies on the Pacific Ocean. At its widest point, Costa Rica spans roughly 174 miles (280 kilometers) from coast to coast. Its narrowest point is only 74 miles (119 km) wide. Covering 19,730 square miles (51,100 square kilometers), Costa Rica is slightly smaller than the state of West Virginia.

Despite its small size, Costa Rica is blessed with highly diverse natural landscapes. They include stunning beaches, lush rain forests, and majestic mountain ranges. The main geographical regions of Costa Rica are the mountains, the Central Valley, the coasts, and the islands.

Opposite: **Manuel Antonio National Park on the Pacific coast is renowned for its white-sand beaches and thick green forests.**

The Mountains

Several major mountain chains make up the interior highlands of Costa Rica. The mountain ranges form the spine of the country, curving from the northwest to the southeast. The northernmost is the Guanacaste Range, which begins near Nicaragua. The Guanacaste is dominated by a towering volcanic peak called Rincón de la Vieja, which reaches 6,217 feet (1,895 m). A smaller range, the Tilarán, lies to the southeast. One of Costa Rica's most active volcanoes, Arenal, is located there.

Gas billows from a vent near a lake atop Poás Volcano. The volcano has not had a major eruption since 1954.

The Active Earth

Costa Rica is located in an area where two plates of the earth's outer layer meet. These boundaries between plates are the parts of the globe that are the most likely to experience earthquakes. The most devastating earthquake in Costa Rican history occurred in the early evening hours of May 4, 1910, leveling the historic city of Cartago (below), near San José. An estimated one thousand people were killed, and most of the buildings in the town were destroyed. The quake also devastated the nearby towns of Orosi and Paraíso.

Volcanoes are another fascinating—and deadly—geological feature of the Costa Rican landscape. The country is part of the Ring of Fire, a line of volcanoes that circles the Pacific Ocean. Costa Rica has six active volcanoes: Arenal (above), Irazú, Poás, Rincón de la Vieja, Turrialba, and Tenorio. Each has erupted in modern times. The most devastating modern eruption occurred in July 1968, when Arenal spewed lava, ash, and rocks for several days. Seventy-eight people were killed and three small villages were buried in ash and volcanic material. Arenal is one of the most active volcanoes on the planet.

The Central Range, in the middle of Costa Rica, also features several active volcanoes. Poás at 8,870 feet (2,704 m) and Irazú at 11,257 feet (3,431) are the main features of two national parks. Adventurous tourists visit the parks to witness the volcanoes' displays of ash, smoke, and glowing orange-red lava being ejected high into the air. Geysers at Poás Volcano spew steam and muddy water hundreds of feet into the sky. It is believed to be the largest geyser system in the world.

Several national parks are located in the towering Talamanca Mountains. La Amistad International Park is split between Costa Rica and Panama. Its name means "friendship" in Spanish.

The rugged Talamanca Range runs from central Costa Rica to the Panama border. Then it continues through Panama and into Colombia. It is Costa Rica's largest and highest mountain range. Chirripó Grande, on the western edge of the Talamancas, is the country's highest point, soaring to 12,530 feet (3,819 m). Another peak, Cerro de la Muerte (Mountain of Death), reaches more than 11,300 feet (3,440 m) high. A lower range of mountains called the Fila Costeña, or Coastal Row, separates the Talamanca Range from the Pacific Ocean. A long fertile valley lies between the Talamancas and the Coastal Row.

Some of Costa Rica's mountain ranges are home to cloud forests. These are forests at elevations from about 3,300 feet to 9,800 feet (1,000 m to 3,000 m) that are almost constantly bathed in clouds. The moist clouds soak the forest with a continual mist. The nourishing environment creates a rich habitat for many plant and animal species.

Costa Rica's Geographic Features

Area: 19,730 square miles (51,100 sq km)

Highest Elevation: Chirripó Grande, 12,530 feet (3,819 m) above sea level

Lowest elevation: Sea level along the coasts

Longest River: San Juan, 140 miles (225 km)

Largest Lake: Arenal, 33 square miles (85 sq km)

Largest City (2011 est.): San José, population 335,000

Average Daily High Temperature: 80°F (27°C) in San José; 86°F (30°C) in Puerto Limón

Average Daily Low Temperature: 65°F (18°C) in San José; 71°F (22°C) in Puerto Limón

Average Annual Rainfall: Caribbean Lowlands, 150 to 200 inches (380 to 500 cm); Central Valley and mountains, 70 inches (180 cm); Pacific coast, 130 inches (330 cm)

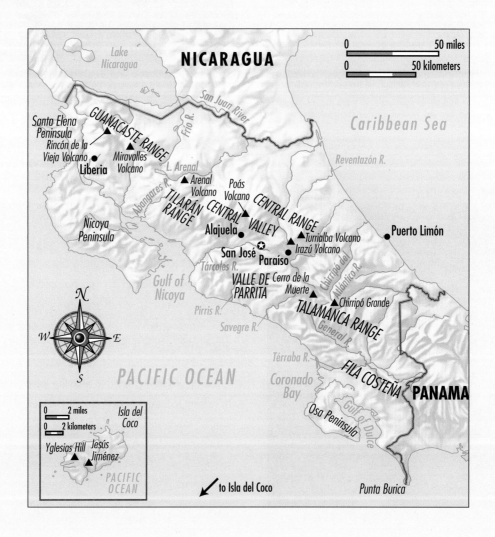

Disappearing Rain Forests

One of Costa Rica's greatest natural wonders is its expanse of tropical rain forests. The forests are home to the richest and most biologically diverse ecosystems in the world. Thousands of plant, bird, butterfly, reptile, amphibian, and mammal species live in the forests.

In the last century, however, more than 80 percent of the forests have been cut down to clear land for agriculture—mainly growing bananas and coffee—cattle ranching, and logging. Cutting the rain forests (below) has resulted in significant soil erosion, because without plant roots to hold the soil in place, it is washed away by the rain. The soil washes into rivers and streams, harming the plants and wildlife that live there, too.

The Costa Rican government has established many conservation programs to slow the tide of deforestation. In 1986, the government founded the National Bamboo Project. This program aimed to reduce deforestation by replacing precious hardwoods with fast-growing, easily replenished bamboo as the main building material in the country. In 1996, the Payments for Environmental Services Program was established. Under it, the government pays landowners to plant trees in deforested areas and to refrain from cutting down trees.

Although deforestation has not ended, the government's conservation efforts seem to be paying off. Since the 1990s, deforestation rates have declined. Private organizations and businesses have joined the government in preservation and reforestation efforts. Many Costa Ricans lend a hand in planting trees (above). The remaining forests, however, are still threatened, mainly by logging companies. These companies continue to clear Costa Rica's forests illegally—and sometimes legally, because logging permits are easy to obtain. Today, the government is working to tighten its regulations and set aside the funds necessary to enforce them.

The Central Valley

The Central Valley is formed at the meeting point of the Central Range and the Talamanca Range. Its area covers about one-fifth of all of Costa Rica but is home to 70 percent of the people. Most major cities, including the capital, San José, are situated in the Central Valley. A mild climate, heavy rainfall, and rich volcanic soil help create plentiful vegeta-

Pineapples and many other crops grow in Costa Rica's Central Valley.

Horseback riding is a fantastic way to enjoy Costa Rica.

tion in the Central Valley. Most of the country's agriculture is located in this region. The main crop grown there is coffee.

The General Valley lies farther south. This region is more rugged. Hills, woodlands, pastures, and farms cover the area.

The Coasts

Costa Rica's jagged Pacific coast extends for about 780 miles (1,250 km). It features miles of white-sand beaches, steep cliffs, and many peninsulas, gulfs, and islands. The Nicoya Peninsula, the nation's largest peninsula, is located in the north. The area is dry and has hilly terrain that is good for cattle farming. The Osa Peninsula lies in the south. This area is home to many banana plantations as well as Corcovado National Park, which protects a rain forest.

The Caribbean coast is much shorter than the Pacific coast, at only about 132 miles (212 km) long. Unlike the rugged terrain found along the Pacific, the land here is mostly flat plains and beaches of

Looking at Costa Rica's Cities

San José, the capital of Costa Rica, is also its largest city, with an estimated population of 335,000 in 2011. Puerto Limón (below), Costa Rica's second-largest city, has a population of 63,080. Located on the Caribbean coast, it is the nation's major commercial port and cruise ship destination. Philipp Valentini, a German-born explorer and archaeologist, officially founded Limón in 1854. The growth of the city was largely the result of the construction of a railroad in the 1870s to serve the booming banana industry. Today, millions of pounds of bananas are shipped through the city every year to locations around the world. Limón is hot and wet throughout the year, with heavy and frequent rainfall. Visitors often stop at the Veragua Rainforest Park, a complex that features a reptile and snake zoo, and gardens that are home to butterflies and hummingbirds.

The nation's third-largest city, Alajuela (above), has a population of 47,494. Agriculture is the main industry in this bustling city in the Central Valley, and coffee, corn, sugarcane, and beans are its chief products. In recent years, heavy industry companies have set up shop in the city. Many visitors enjoy the Juan Santamaría Museum of Cultural History, which commemorates Santamaría, Costa Rica's national hero, who was born in Alajuela.

Founded in 1769 as a settlement where religious people lived in seclusion, Liberia is Costa Rica's fourth-largest city, with a population of 45,380. Liberia is noted for its colonial architecture, with narrow streets, old adobe (mud brick) homes, and charming central plaza. The Church of La Ermita de la Agonía, built in 1865, is the only remaining colonial-era church in the northwest. Its whitewashed adobe walls and clay roof and floor tiles are vivid reminders of a once-dominant architectural style.

black sand and white sand. Several areas of lowlands in the north have volcanoes and a few hills. In recent years, the Caribbean coast has developed into a popular surfing and tourist destination. Tortuguero National Park and Cahuita National Park offer nature lovers a chance to see turtle nesting grounds and colorful coral reefs.

Islands

Costa Rica's Pacific coast features a scattering of islands. Some islands are inhabited and others are maintained as biological reserves. Tortuga Island in the Gulf of Nicoya is a major tourist attraction, visited for its beautiful beaches. Nearby San Lucas Island was used as a prison during the nineteenth and twentieth centuries. Today, visitors can wander the ruins of the jail and glimpse wildlife, such as howler monkeys, deer, pheasants, and bats. Off the Osa Peninsula, Isla del Caño and the surrounding waters are a biological reserve featuring many species of sea turtles, dolphins, and whales.

Isla del Coco lies in the Pacific Ocean, 364 miles (586 km) off the coast. The uninhabited island features rugged terrain marked by mountains, forests, towering cliffs, and waterfalls. The island is a national park, home to 235 species of plants, 362 species of insects, and about two hundred species of fish. Because of the abundant sea life, the waters off Isla del Coco are considered some of the best scuba diving spots in the world. Legends claim that pirates often buried treasures on Isla del Coco. To date, hundreds of attempts to find the buried fortunes have failed.

Rivers and Lakes

Many rivers and streams flow throughout Costa Rica. Most of them originate in the mountains. The Río Grande de Tárcoles and the Río Grande de Térraba, two of the country's largest rivers, flow into the Pacific. The San Juan River and the Reventazón River are the main rivers that flow into the Caribbean. The San Juan originates in Nicaragua and forms a large part of Costa Rica's border with that country. Smaller rivers include the Pirris, Abangares, and the Savegre, which flow through the banana plantations in the Central Valley.

Lake Arenal, Costa Rica's largest lake, is located in the northern highlands near Arenal Volcano. It is a reservoir, or artificial lake, which was formed by damming the Arenal River. This dam is part of a hydroelectric project that supplies

A scuba diver swims among countless colorful fish off Isla del Coco.

Lake Arenal is considered one of the world's best windsurfing spots.

about 17 percent of the country's electricity. From November through April, strong winds blow across the lake, and windsurfers flock there to enjoy a day on the water.

Climate

Costa Rica lies near the equator, an imaginary line that circles the globe halfway between the North and the South Poles. Like all places near the equator, Costa Rica is warm year-round. Still, Costa Rica experiences a wide variety of weather. There are two basic seasons: *invierno*, the wet season, and *verano*, the dry season. The wet season lasts from May to November. The dry season lasts from December to April.

The Caribbean Lowlands experience heavy rainfall almost all year long, as northeasterly winds bring moist air from the warm waters of the sea. Average annual rainfall in the lowlands and the eastern slopes of the highlands average about 150 to 200 inches (380 to 500 centimeters) a year. Daytime temperatures can hit 100°F (38°C). The plentiful rainfall and high temperatures provide ideal growing conditions for bananas and other fruit. The Pacific coast receives about 130 inches (330 cm) of rainfall each year. Like the Caribbean Lowlands, the climate is ideal for growing bananas and other fruit.

The mountains and higher regions of the Central Valley experience less rainfall and generally have a more moderate climate. An average of 70 inches (180 cm) of rain falls each year. Daytime temperatures average roughly 75°F (24°C).

The Caribbean coast is the wettest region of Costa Rica. During the wet season, rain drenches the region almost every afternoon.

CHAPTER 3

Magnificent Life

OSTA RICA IS BURSTING WITH AN AMAZING VARIETY of plant and animal life. It is estimated that Costa Rica is home to about a half million species of plants and animals. This represents about 4 percent of the total species on Earth. Costa Rica's incredible diversity of wildlife is largely the result of its location. Since Central America forms a land bridge connecting North and South America, plant and animal species from both continents migrated across the land. Many also settled in what is now Costa Rica. New species continue to be found today.

Forests and Vegetation

There are more than two thousand different species of trees and nine thousand types of flowering plants in Costa Rica. Many of these species are found in Costa Rica's two types of tropical forests: tropical dry forests and tropical rain forests.

National Flower

The *guaria morada* is Costa Rica's national flower. It is a member of the orchid family and is prized by flower lovers for its vibrant purple colors and bright shimmer. The guaria morada grows mainly along the Pacific coast and in low-lying mountain regions. Many Costa Rican families grow the colorful flower in their yards and proudly display it at orchid shows.

Tropical dry forests surround the Gulf of Nicoya and the Pacific coast along the Nicoya Peninsula. Drought conditions in the region last from about November to April. Because of the lack of rainfall, tropical dry forests are not as thickly forested as tropical rain forests. Average rainfall during the year is about 45 to 60 inches (110 to 150 cm). During the dry season, fire is a major danger for the forests. When the rains come, leafy trees such as the purple jacaranda and orange flame of the forest burst into vivid colors.

Tropical rain forests are found throughout the north, along the Caribbean coast, and in the central and southern lowlands. Average annual rainfall ranges from 80 to 235 inches (200 to 600 cm). The year-round rainfall, long hours of sunlight, and high temperatures and humidity create ideal conditions for plant life. The most common rain forest trees are tall evergreens. Orchids, mosses, and lichens grow on the ground below.

Costa Rica's coastlines feature palm trees and mangroves. Palm trees grow in abundance on the Caribbean coast. They have also been transplanted to the Pacific Lowlands.

Mangroves are unusual trees because they are able to grow in salty coastal water. They are found mainly along the Gulf of Nicoya and the Gulf of Dulce. Seven different species of mangrove live in Costa Rica. With their fingerlike, interlocking roots that reach into the water, mangroves provide a home to many marine animals such as fish, oysters, crabs, and lobsters.

The tangle of mangrove roots creates a safe nursery for young fish and other creatures.

National Tree

The guanacaste is Costa Rica's national tree. It is sometimes called the "ear tree" because of the brown, elephant-ear-shaped seedpods that hang high in the tree. Guanacaste wood is used in high-quality carpentry and crafts. The sap of the tree is often used as a cold medicine. Grazing cattle feed on the guanacaste's branches, leaves, and fruit. The seeds of the guanacaste fruit are often used to make jewelry.

Amphibians and Reptiles

Costa Rica is home to about 175 species of amphibians, most of them frogs. The most common species of frogs are the red-eyed tree frog and the poison dart frog. There are many types of toads, including the giant toad, which can grow up to 6 inches (15 cm) long and weigh as much as 4.4 pounds (2 kilograms). More than forty species of salamanders live in Costa Rica, and they are all lungless. Instead of breathing with lungs, they take in air through their skin. Costa Rica is also home to two species of caecilians, an amphibian that looks like an earthworm.

An estimated 225 species of reptiles live in Costa Rica. This includes more than seventy types of lizards and about 120 species of snakes. The black iguana and green iguana are

Despite their name, green iguanas come in many colors. They eat mostly plants and spend most of their time in trees.

among the most common reptiles. They are often farmed as a source of food and an export for the pet industry. Costa Rica has about twenty poisonous snakes, including two species of bushmasters, the longest poisonous snakes in the Western Hemisphere. They can grow to 10 feet (3 m) long. Sea turtles are found in the Caribbean Lowlands. The American crocodile and its smaller relative, the spectacled caiman, live in the wet lowlands on both coasts.

Fruit accounts for more than half the food eaten by white-faced capuchin monkeys. Their favorite fruits include mangoes and figs.

Mammals

Costa Rica is home to about 250 species of mammals, half of which are bats. Costa Rican bats include the Honduran white bat and the large spectral bat, which hunts and feeds on small birds and small animals, including other bats. Monkey species include the white-headed capuchin and the mantled howler. The loud howling noises that the mantled howlers make help the members within a group find one another. Sloths, coatis,

National Animal

The white-tailed deer is the national animal of Costa Rica. Adult white-tailed deer have reddish-brown coats in summer. In winter, their coats turn grayish brown. Only male deer, or bucks, grow antlers. White-tailed deer eat leaves, fruits and nuts, and corn. They are speedy runners and highly agile. They can sprint up to 30 miles (50 km) per hour and leap as high as 10 feet (3 m) and as far as 30 feet (9 m) in a single jump.

which are related to raccoons, and playful but fierce weasel-like creatures called tayras are also found in Costa Rica's forests.

Six members of the cat family are found in Costa Rica. They are jaguars, pumas, ocelots, oncillas, jaguarundis, and margays. Some cat species have been hunted to near extinction, while others are endangered. Jaguars are the largest cats in Costa Rica, growing up to 6 feet (2 m) long. Pumas are the second-largest cat. Oncillas, also called little spotted cats, grow to about the size of a house cat and live in cloud forests.

Birds

About nine hundred species of birds have been found in Costa Rica. More than two-thirds of them live in Costa Rica year-round, while the rest migrate from outside the country. The endangered resplendent quetzal eats fruit, insects, and small lizards. The quetzal makes remarkable calls that echo in its cloud forest habitat. The brightly colored scarlet macaw, once common in Costa Rica's forests, is also endangered. Fortunately, both of these birds are found in large numbers in protected nature reserves such as the Monteverde Cloud Forest and Chirripó National Park. Other colorful birds include toucans, hummingbirds, parrots, and tanagers.

Insects, Butterflies, and Moths

Several thousand species of insects live in Costa Rica, although many more have not yet been identified. Beetles, leaf-cutter ants, bees, and katydids (a type of cricket) are among the insects found there. The country has more than 1,250 species of butterflies and about eight thousand species of moths. Ten percent of the butterfly species in the world live in Costa Rica. The morpho butterfly and the green page moth are two of the most common species found in Costa Rica.

Morpho butterflies are often colored a metallic blue or green.

Sea Life

With roughly 900 miles (1,450 km) of coastline, Costa Rica supports a rich diversity of sea life. The endangered leatherback sea turtle nests at Tortuguero National Park on the Caribbean Sea and at Playa Grande on the Nicoya Peninsula on the Pacific coast. The leatherback is the world's largest sea turtle. It can reach up to 8 feet (2.4 km) in length and weigh more than 1,200 pounds (545 kg). The green turtle and the olive ridley turtle are other common turtles found in Costa Rica.

A sea turtle heads back out to sea after laying eggs at Tortuguero National Park.

Whale sharks, which grow to 45 feet (14 m) in length, are frequently spotted off Isla del Coco. Moray eels inhabit rocky areas and reefs on both coasts, coming out at night to hunt for small fish, shrimp, and octopus. Humpback whales are often seen off Costa Rica's southern Pacific coast at Drake Bay and Isla del Caño. Playful bottle-nosed dolphins are found along both coasts and in the Gulf of Dulce. Manta rays are found along the Pacific coast. The manta is the largest species of ray. These large, kite-shaped creatures sometimes reach 20 feet (6 m) across and weigh more than 3,000 pounds (1,360 km). Brain coral, which looks like a human brain, grows in reefs off both coasts.

Scuba divers get a close look at a whale shark off Isla del Coco. Whale sharks are the world's largest living fish species.

National Parks

The amazing diversity of plant and animal life can best be seen in many of Costa Rica's national parks. Two of the country's most notable national parks are Chirripó and Barra Honda.

Chirripó National Park lies in the Talamanca Range and surrounds Costa Rica's highest mountain, Chirripó Grande. It is one of the most biologically diverse areas in the world. The differences in soil, climate, altitude, and land formations produce huge habitat extremes. No trees grow in *páramo* ecosystems, which are desolate high-altitude areas. Instead, the páramo features rugged shrubs and grasses. Cloud forests include large trees such as oak, sweet cedar, nargusta, and magnolia. In these constantly damp regions, mosses and ferns cover the trees, and orchids grow in abundance. In lower elevations, groves of Lomaria fern and sphagnum moss can be found. Swamplands are filled with herbs and shrubby grasses.

Hundreds of animal species live in Chirripó National Park. More than four hundred species of birds are found there, ranging from the tiny volcano hummingbird to the majestic crested eagle. Colorful birds include the quetzal and the long-tailed motmot. All members of the wildcat family that live in Costa Rica are found in the park. The park also features Costa Rica's largest concentration of tapirs, which are pig-shaped mammals with short snouts. Monkeys and cacomistles, small raccoon-like creatures, also make their home in the park.

Barra Honda National Park is located about 200 miles (300 km) northwest of San José. Its main feature is a huge system of underground caves that plunge as deep as 816 feet (249 m). The caves are home to bats, fish, blind salamanders, and specialized plants that can grow without sunlight.

Barra Honda is surrounded by thick forests of wild plum, gumbo-limbo, wild cotton, and gonçalo alves, which is often

Monteverde Cloud Forest Reserve

The Monteverde Cloud Forest Reserve is located in northern Costa Rica in the Tilarán Range. In the 1950s, members of an American religious group known as Quakers purchased land in Costa Rica to farm. Biologists visiting the area in the 1960s recommended to the Quakers that the lush forests of the region be preserved. The Quakers created a nature preserve and bought additional land. In the 1970s the area

was given its current name, and it formally became a reserve dedicated to scientific research.

Today the Monteverde Cloud Forest Reserve covers more than 26,000 acres (10,500 hectares) and contains amazing biodiversity. There are more than 2,500 plant species, four hundred bird species, one hundred mammal species, 120 reptile and amphibian species, and tens of thousands of insect species. Among the natural treasures found at the reserve are more than four hundred types of orchids.

Tens of thousands of tourists visit the Monteverde Cloud Forest Reserve each year. Visitors can walk the many trails in the park—including some built in the treetops—and marvel at the incredible diversity of plant and animal life.

called zebrawood or tigerwood because of its unique pattern of streaks. Yellow grasshoppers, armadillos, orange-fronted parakeets, and white-faced capuchin monkeys share the forests. Like so many places in Costa Rica, the rich habitat at Barra Honda shelters a wealth of magnificent life.

CHAPTER 4

Independence and Peace

THE FIRST PEOPLES TO INHABIT THE REGION OF present-day Costa Rica were nomadic hunter-gatherers. They arrived in the area as early as 12,000 BCE. They lived in the forests and valleys, hunting small game and collecting edible plants, such as nuts and fruits. Many also fished along the rivers and coastlines. By roughly 2000 BCE people who had migrated to the region from both the north and the south began growing crops such as corn, sweet potatoes, beans, and squash. They lived in large communities, mainly in the Central Valley and in the northern Pacific coast region.

Establishing Trade

These communities established trade networks with Mayan peoples and other groups from the north. As early as 800 BCE, people in the northern areas of Guanacaste and Nicoya were trading with people in what are now Mexico and Guatemala. Artifacts found in northwestern Costa Rica, such as jade, ceramic, and gold items, reflect distinct Mayan influences. Other northern influences included growing corn and beans.

Early Costa Rican peoples also traded and interacted with groups as far south as the Andes Mountains, in what is now Ecuador, in South America. The communities of what is now southern Costa Rica began to grow cassava, an edible root, and chew coca leaves, an Andean custom.

When Europeans first arrived in Costa Rica in the early sixteenth century, an estimated four hundred thousand people lived in the immediate area. There were many different groups of indigenous peoples. Among the largest of the groups were the Chorotegas, who inhabited Guanacaste in the northwest. The Diquís people lived in the southwest, the Caribs in the southern Caribbean region, and the Corobicis in the Central Valley and highlands.

The Diquís people were accomplished goldsmiths. This religious figure is between five hundred and one thousand years old.

Mysterious Spheres

Costa Rica is home to one of the world's greatest archaeological mysteries. Near the Diquís River and on Isla del Caño sit more than three hundred solid rock spheres, or balls, made of granite, gabbro, limestone, and sandstone. Most of the rocks stand in fields or alongside roads. Others are grouped near ancient cemeteries. Some sit on a bed made of cobblestone. The spheres range in size from a few inches in diameter to more than 6.5 feet (2 m) in diameter. Some of the larger rocks weigh as much as 16 tons (14.5 metric tons).

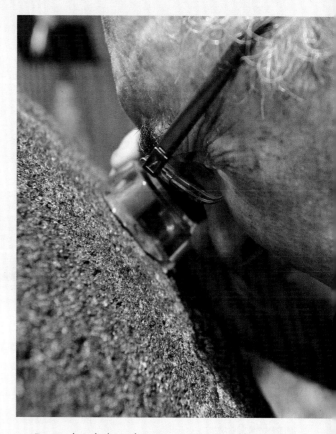

Researchers believe the stones were carved between 200 BCE and 1500 CE. Excavation crews from the United Fruit Company discovered the spheres in the 1930s when they were clearing the jungle for banana plantations. Workers who believed gold might have been hidden in the stones destroyed many spheres by drilling into them or blowing them up with dynamite. Many of the spheres are on display at the National Museum of Costa Rica in San José. Some of them have been moved to the entrances of government buildings.

There are many theories about why these balls were made. Some experts have suggested they were cemetery markers, while others say they have something to do with a calendar. But to this day, no one knows for sure.

Christopher Columbus (standing) convinced Spain's King Ferdinand and Queen Isabella to fund his journey across the Atlantic Ocean.

The Europeans Arrive

Italian explorer Christopher Columbus was the first European to reach Costa Rica. In 1502, leading his fourth and last trip to the Western Hemisphere, he landed at Uvita Island, near what is now Puerto Limón, on the Caribbean coast. Columbus reported to Spain's king Ferdinand, who sponsored his voyage, that the indigenous people wore gold jewelry and gave him gifts of gold.

Eager to find the large reserves of the precious mineral, Spain sent more explorers to the region. In 1522, Gil González Dávila explored most of the Pacific coast. Several years later, Francisco Hernández de Córdoba founded Bruselas, the first Spanish settlement in Costa Rica. It was located near what is now Puntarenas, on the Gulf of Nicoya. Excited by the prospects of gold, the Spaniards began calling the region Costa Rica, which means "rich coast" in Spanish.

Guayabo National Monument

The Guayabo National Monument is the largest and most important archaeological site in Costa Rica. Located about 12 miles (19 km) northeast of Turrialba, in the center of the country, Guayabo was home to as many as ten thousand people between 1000 BCE and 1500 CE. Archaeologists do not know why the city was abandoned. Scientists have found paved streets, bridges, temple foundations, and a large system of aqueducts that supplied water to the city's residents. Most of the ruins are still waiting to be uncovered, providing hope that further excavations will reveal more about the ancient history of Guayabo.

Later Spanish expeditions, however, found very little gold. The Spanish turned their attention to establishing settlements in Costa Rica. In 1561 Juan de Cavallón founded Garcimuñoz. Then in 1563 Juan Vásquez de Coronado founded Cartago in the Central Valley and made it the capital of the province.

Colonial Costa Rica

The indigenous people did not welcome the Spanish intruders. They resisted the Spanish invasion, but their weapons were no match for the Europeans' horses, guns, and iron weapons. Many indigenous people were captured, enslaved,

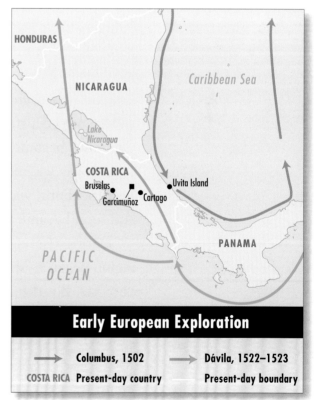

Early European Exploration

→ Columbus, 1502 → Dávila, 1522–1523
COSTA RICA Present-day country —— Present-day boundary

and forced to work in the Spanish colonies. Thousands died from smallpox, measles, typhoid fever, and other diseases that came with the Spaniards to the Western Hemisphere. The indigenous people had never before been exposed to these diseases, so their bodies could not fight them off. Many indigenous people fled into distant forested areas to avoid being captured by the Spaniards.

The Spanish settlers started farms. If there were not enough indigenous people nearby to work on their farms, they hired mestizo children, the children of Spanish men and indigenous women, and treated them as virtual slaves. Corn, sugarcane, tobacco, and beans were grown on these farms. Spanish farmers also raised livestock, such as cattle and pigs. In Costa Rica, large plantations did not develop. Instead, smaller farms were common.

Costa Rica grew slowly throughout the seventeenth and eighteenth centuries. Gradually, towns were established. Churches became an important part of daily life. The town of Cartago was destroyed in 1723 by the eruption of Irazú Volcano, but it was later rebuilt. San José was founded in 1737 and soon became the major city of the province.

During the eighteenth century, Spain's control over the region began to slip. Spain established laws for all its colonial outposts. But the laws were often impossible to enforce, especially in Costa Rica, because the province was so remote and isolated. The local colonial governors were more concerned with their own survival than carrying out the orders of the Spanish crown thousands of miles away.

Independence

Mexico gained its independence from Spain in August 1821. At that time, Costa Rica, Nicaragua, El Salvador, Honduras, and Guatemala also declared themselves independent from Spain. In 1823 the five countries joined together in a federation called the United Provinces of Central America.

From the beginning, the United Provinces suffered from a lack of common goals and interests. Costa Rica and Nicaragua quarreled over the region of Guanacaste. There was constant political struggle between the rich landowners and the common people.

Central Americans celebrate winning their independence from Spain, and becoming a united federation in 1823.

The federation slowly began to dissolve. Costa Rica became independent in 1838, and the federation ceased entirely in 1840.

Although the United Provinces of Central America failed, it did offer the region a model for a republic, a government in which leaders are elected. Each state in the federation had an elected president, a senate, and a supreme court. Slavery was abolished, as were the privileges of the clergy and nobility. Many of these democratic ideals helped shape Costa Rica in the future.

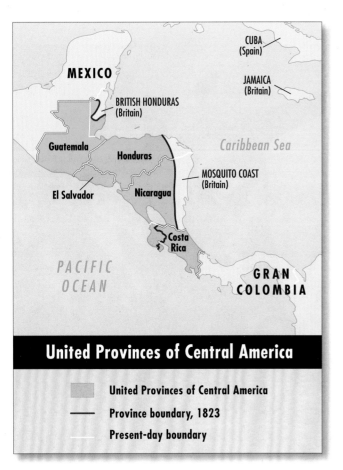

United Provinces of Central America

- United Provinces of Central America
- Province boundary, 1823
- Present-day boundary

The Early Years

Costa Rica's first few decades of independence were unstable. In its first forty-five years of self-rule, twenty-two men held power. Juan Mora Fernández was elected the country's first president, in 1824. He ruled peacefully for nine years. Fernández expanded public education and established the nation's first judicial system. He also encouraged the cultivation of coffee as an export crop by offering free land to new growers. In 1843, the first shipment of Costa Rican coffee was sent to England. By 1850, Costa Rica was Europe's largest coffee supplier. Costa Rica's coffee barons, the men who controlled the coffee industry, came to dominate Costa Rica.

The Strange Story of William Walker

William Walker was an American adventurer from Tennessee. He was highly educated, with degrees in law and medicine. Walker proposed that the United States conquer Central America, establish slavery there, and create new slaveholding states. Wealthy American industrialist Cornelius Vanderbilt and a group of U.S. slaveholders provided Walker with substantial financial support.

In 1855, Walker and his army invaded Nicaragua, which was involved in a civil war. He took control of the Nicaraguan army and declared himself president.

Walker then set his sights on invading Costa Rica. Costa Rican president Juan Rafael Mora, however, raised an army of nine thousand to combat the threat. In 1856, they marched to the Nicaraguan border, where Walker's men attacked them. In the Battle of Rivas, the Costa Ricans routed Walker's army and chased them back into Nicaragua. Many Costa Rican soldiers died in the battle. A drummer boy named Juan Santamaría became a national hero by setting fire to an enemy position before he was shot and killed.

Walker continued to make trouble in Central America for several years. In 1860, he was executed by a Honduran firing squad after he attempted to seize control of Honduras.

In 1870, General Tomás Guardia overthrew the government and became president. He served for the next twelve years. He disbanded the congress and created a new constitution for the country in 1871.

Although Guardia was a harsh military ruler, he had many progressive ideas. Guardia placed high taxes on the rich coffee growers and used the money to improve public health, education, and transportation. He also abolished the death penalty and improved the nation's network of roads.

Railroads and Bananas

One of Guardia's most important contributions was building a railroad that connected San José to Puerto Limón on the Caribbean coast. The railroad was built to transport coffee from the highlands to the country's main port. In 1871, Guardia hired a U.S. company to build the railroad. An American named Minor Cooper Keith was chosen to lead the project. Progress was painfully slow at first. Clearing the rain forest was very difficult. Thousands of workers died from diseases such as malaria and yellow fever.

Most Costa Rican men did not want to work on the railroad because of its deadly reputation. Keith brought in Chinese and Jamaican laborers to complete the task. He also took on convicts from jails in New Orleans. About five thousand people died during the construction, including Keith's uncle and both of his brothers.

The Costa Rican government gave Keith's company vast tracts of land along the railroad. During the railroad's construction, Keith started growing bananas on this land. Costa Rica's untouched forests were turned into banana plantations. The banana business was an enormous success and made Keith a wealthy man. In 1899, Keith's company combined with another to become the United Fruit Company. This company became extraordinarily powerful in Costa Rica. It had so much influence on the economy, government, and other aspects of society that it became known as *el pulpo*, the octopus.

Piles of bananas ready to be loaded onto a railroad owned by the United Fruit Company. In the early twentieth century, Costa Rica was the world's leading exporter of bananas.

Democracy and Dictators

After President Guardia died in 1882, a group called the Generation of 1888 continued his work. In 1890, José Joaquin Rodriguez was elected president. It was the first time since the 1840s that someone not supported by the rich coffee growers took office. Many consider it the first free and honest election in Central America. Democracy was still limited, however. Only men could vote. Indigenous people and people of African and Chinese descent were also barred from voting.

In the following decades, democratic ideals generally continued to spread. Social programs and public works programs were expanded, and religious freedoms were put in place. Under

The Pacific Railroad connecting San José to Puntarenas on the Pacific coast was completed in 1910.

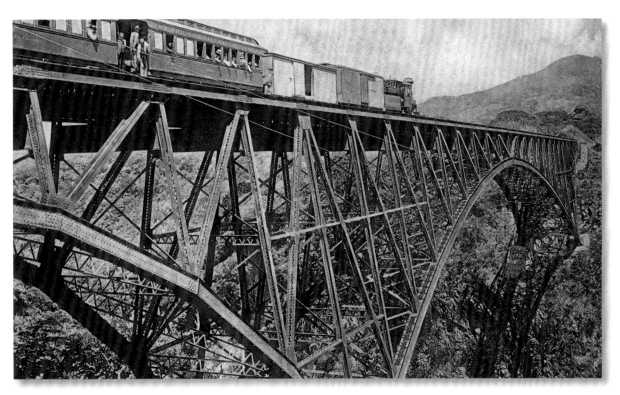

Cleto González Víquez, who served as president from 1906 to 1910 and 1928 to 1932, health care was improved, streets were paved in San José, and railroads were completed. Ricardo Jiménez Oreamuno served as president three times—from 1910 to 1914, 1924 to 1928, and 1932 to 1936. During his time in office, Jiménez tried to improve the voting system. Both of these presidents required that lands the government had given to Minor Keith's company be redistributed to the poor.

Costa Rica's economy slumped during World War I (1914–1918). Exports of bananas and coffee declined, and the national debt increased. In 1917, during this uncertain time, President Alfredo González Flores, a liberal, was overthrown by his minister of war, Federico Tinoco. The new president limited freedom of the press and violated Costa Ricans' civil rights. Those who opposed him were rounded up and jailed.

By the 1920s, San José was peppered with grand buildings.

Federico Tinoco was an authoritarian leader who was widely disliked. He remained in power only two years.

Costa Ricans responded forcefully to Tinoco's repressive regime. Schoolteachers, mostly women, and high school students organized and rebelled. They set fire to a pro-Tinoco newspaper plant. Government troops were sent in to put down the uprising, but they fired into the U.S. consulate, where some demonstrators were hiding. The U.S. government threatened to intervene in the trouble. Finally, the Costa Rican congress forced Tinoco to resign and flee the country. Tinoco's dictatorship was the last in Costa Rican history.

Civil War

For decades Costa Ricans enjoyed the benefits of education, civil rights, and a stable government. But by the mid-twentieth century, most people remained poor. Jobs were difficult to find, housing was expensive, and workers were not paid well. Costa Ricans looked to their leaders for help.

Rafael Ángel Calderón Guardia was elected president in 1940 with 85 percent of the vote. He quickly introduced social reforms and labor laws to benefit the working class. He created an insurance fund that gave benefits to disabled workers and working women who were having babies. He fought for a national wage increase and recognized the workers' right to strike. Soon, however, business leaders and the middle class became outraged at Calderón's liberal programs. They accused him of fraud and corruption. By 1948, Costa Rica had become politically unstable. Violent protests and assassinations began to tear apart the nation.

Calderón had two main opponents: Otilio Ulate Blanco, a newspaper publisher, and José Figueres Ferrer, a rich landowner. Ulate, representing the National Union Party, ran against Calderón in the 1948 election. Ulate won by more than ten thousand votes over Calderón, who was running as the National Republican Party candidate. Each side accused the other of rigging the election. Costa Rica's Election Commission concluded that the Legislative Assembly should decide the outcome of the election. The assembly, filled with Calderón supporters, appointed Calderón president.

Ulate did not accept the legislature's decision. An armed force of volunteers soon came to his support. José Figueres Ferrer led this antigovernment army, made up mostly of students and sons of farmers. Nicaraguan president General Anastasio Somoza García then sent forces to northern Costa Rica in support of Calderón.

The government forces were poorly trained and unable to defeat Figueres's revolutionaries. The volunteers, called the

National Liberation Army, soon gained control of Cartago, Puerto Limón, and San José. The fighting lasted about five weeks, during which time about two thousand people were killed. Calderón fled the country.

Figueres became the temporary leader of the country and governed for eighteen months. A new constitution was adopted in 1949. It gave women and people of African descent the right to vote, reformed elections, and abolished the army. Figueres's actions put Costa Rica on the path to becoming a real democracy. During this time, Figueres also started putting more money into social programs, especially education and health. In 1949, Figueres handed over leadership of Costa Rica to Ulate and the legislature as promised.

José Figueres Ferrer faced several rebellions during his early time in power. Here, he is surrounded by victorious troops after the surrender of the rebels.

Father of the New Costa Rica

José Figueres Ferrer, affectionately called Don Pepe, is known as the father of the new Costa Rica. He was born in 1906 after his parents arrived in Costa Rica from Spain. During the 1920s, he studied engineering in the United States. There, he became fascinated with the U.S. economy and system of government. He returned to Costa Rica, where he bought a farm and experimented with new agricultural techniques and products.

In the 1940s, Figueres criticized President Rafael Ángel Calderón Guardia. He was exiled to Mexico for his outspoken opinions. There he met Otilio Ulate Blanco. After the civil war, Figueres became a national hero to Costa Ricans. He founded the National Liberation Party and was elected president twice. Figueres's belief in democracy helped lead Costa Rica into a period of political stability and economic growth in the mid-twentieth century. He died in 1990 at the age of eighty-three.

New Woes

In 1951, Figueres founded the National Liberation Party, and two years later he was elected president. In 1955, Nicaraguans who supported Figueres's old rival Rafael Ángel Calderón invaded northern Costa Rica. With an army of six thousand volunteers, Figueres fought off the invaders. The conflict ended when the governments of Nicaragua and Costa Rica signed an agreement not to support rebel military forces in each other's country. The treaty temporarily stopped the hostilities, but border disputes, although unarmed, continue to this day.

Figueres was elected again in 1970. By the time he left office four years later, Costa Rica was facing serious economic

Costa Rican president Luis Alberto Monge Álvarez (right) speaks with U.S. president Ronald Reagan in 1982. As president, Monge limited government spending and promoted exports and tourism.

problems. The government was deeply in debt to foreign countries from which it had borrowed money. Oil and fuel prices had skyrocketed worldwide. Civil wars in nearby countries harmed Costa Rican commerce and slowed foreign investment in the region. The price of coffee, the country's main export, had dropped significantly.

The economic troubles continued into the 1980s. Unemployment was high and a drop in wages prevented many people from affording the goods and services they needed. Industrial production had declined. Costa Rica was unable to pay back monies it owed foreign governments and banks.

In 1982, Luis Alberto Monge Álvarez was elected president. Monge secured loans from the International Monetary Fund (IMF), an organization that lends money to struggling nations in exchange for exercising control over their finances. With additional financial aid coming from the United States, Costa Rica began to emerge from its economic crisis in the mid-1980s.

A Threat of War

As Costa Rica battled its economic problems, the possibility of a regional war, brewing from events years earlier, threatened the nation's dedication to peace. In 1979, Nicaraguan dictator Anastasio Somoza Debayle was forced from power. A group called the Sandinistas seized control of the Nicaraguan government. Thousands of Nicaraguans fled to Costa Rica. The United States pressured Costa Rica to let Contras, anti-Sandinista fighters, establish bases in Costa Rica. From there, the Contras would conduct raids into Nicaragua.

In 1986, Óscar Arias Sánchez became president of Costa Rica. He was outraged that his country was dragged into the dangerous conflict with Nicaragua. He reestablished

Sandinista soldiers launch rockets during a battle near the Costa Rican border.

diplomatic relations with Nicaragua and expelled Contras living in Costa Rica. He then negotiated a peace plan to end all hostilities in Central America. The presidents of five nations—Costa Rica, Nicaragua, El Salvador, Guatemala, and Honduras—signed the agreement in August 1987. Arias won the Nobel Peace Prize for his work.

Recent Years

Economic issues once again dominated Costa Rican politics in the 1990s. Rafael Ángel Calderón Fournier, the son of former president Calderón, was elected president in 1990. At the time, Costa Rica was under pressure from the IMF and another organization called the World Bank to shrink government spending and favor private business. To reduce government spending and pay back the country's loans,

Óscar Arias Sánchez meets with Cardinal Miguel Obando y Bravo of Nicaragua during Central American peace talks. Obando y Bravo, the most powerful religious leader in Central America, was an outspoken opponent of the Sandinistas.

San José is now a busy, vibrant city.

Calderón Fournier put many government-owned businesses into private ownership. He also increased taxes and decreased the government's spending on social welfare programs. The IMF and the World Bank also supported the development of a tourist-based economy.

Calderón Fournier's successor, José María Figueres Olsen, the son of former president José Figueres Ferrer, was elected president in 1994. He brought new industries and foreign investment into the country, which increased the nation's manufacturing income. In 2010 Costa Rica elected its first female president, Laura Chinchilla. She had been a vice president in the previous administration.

Costa Ricans have faced many challenges throughout the years, but have remained true to their beliefs in democracy, peace, and education. It remains a hopeful example in an unstable, impoverished region.

CHAPTER 5

Democracy at Work

OSTA RICA IS THE OLDEST DEMOCRATIC REPUBLIC in Central America. It was the first country in the region to hold free and fair elections. Every four years, Costa Ricans elect the president, vice presidents, members of the Legislative Assembly, and local council members. According to law, voting is required by all citizens age eighteen and older. This law is not enforced, however, and the percentage of citizens who vote has declined in recent elections. In the 2010 presidential election, only 69 percent of adults voted. That figure is still higher than the 57 percent of registered voters who took part in the 2012 U.S. presidential election.

National Government

Costa Rica is governed under the 1949 constitution. The constitution has been slightly revised, or amended, twenty-eight times since it was adopted. The constitution divides the government into three branches: executive, legislative, and judicial.

The president is the head of the executive branch. He or she serves a four-year term. To become president, a candidate must receive at least 40 percent of the vote. If no candidate passes that mark, a runoff election is held between the two people with the most votes. The president must be Costa Rican and at least thirty years old.

The president appoints cabinet ministers. Each minister oversees a different government department, such as finance, education, foreign relations, and social welfare. The president also represents the nation in official acts and commands

Laura Chinchilla was elected the first female president of Costa Rica in 2010.

A Visit to San José

San José is the capital of Costa Rica. The city was established in 1737, and in 1823, it replaced Cartago as the nation's capital. In 2011, San José had a population of about 335,000. Although only a small percentage of San José's total population lives in the city center, more than one million people commute into the metropolitan area each day to work.

San José sits in a fertile valley in the Central Range at 3,840 feet (1,170 m) above sea level. Although it lies in a tropical rain forest, its high elevation provides it with a mild, pleasant climate.

The city is home to many important cultural and historic sites. The National Theater, which opened in 1897, was built with money from the nation's tax on coffee. The Jade Museum has the world's largest collection of pre-Columbian jade artifacts dating from 500 BCE to 800 CE. The National Museum (below, right)

is housed in a former army barracks where fighting occurred during the civil war of 1848. Visitors can still see hundreds of bullet holes on the outside walls. The museum features exhibits on Costa Rican history from ancient times to the present.

San José

the security forces. Laura Chinchilla was elected president in 2010. She had previously served as one of President Óscar Arias Sánchez's vice presidents and his administration's minister of justice.

Two vice presidents assist the president. If the president leaves office for any reason, the first vice president becomes president. The second vice president and the president of the Legislative Assembly are next in line.

The Legislative Assembly has fifty-seven members, called deputies. Members must be Costa Rican and at least twenty-

The Costa Rican flag has five horizontal stripes. The top and bottom stripes are dark blue, the middle stripe is red, and the stripes between the red and blue stripes are white. Blue represents democracy and growth in the country. White represents wisdom, happiness, and peace. Red represents the warmth of the people and the blood of their sacrifices. Costa Rica's national emblem, or coat of arms, appears on the red stripe. It features three volcano peaks, sailing ships, and the rising sun. Above the scene are seven stars representing the seven provinces of Costa Rica. The flag was officially adopted in 1906.

one years old. The Legislative Assembly holds the power to make laws, approve the national budget, impose taxes, and authorize the president to declare war.

President Laura Chinchilla speaks to the Legislative Assembly.

National Government of Costa Rica

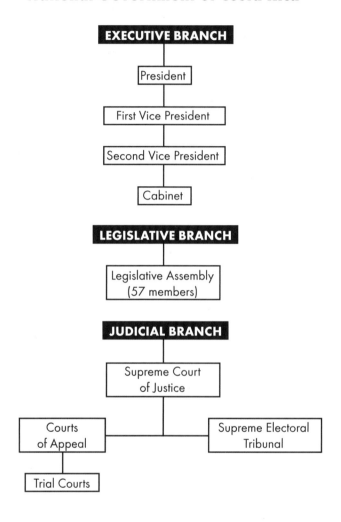

EXECUTIVE BRANCH

President

First Vice President

Second Vice President

Cabinet

LEGISLATIVE BRANCH

Legislative Assembly
(57 members)

JUDICIAL BRANCH

Supreme Court
of Justice

Courts
of Appeal

Supreme Electoral
Tribunal

Trial Courts

The highest court in the land is the Supreme Court of Justice. It is composed of twenty-two judges who are elected by the Legislative Assembly. Judges are elected to terms of eight years and must be at least thirty-five years old. The Supreme Court appoints judges in the lower courts, including the Supreme Electoral Tribunal. The tribunal oversees the nation's

The Supreme Electoral Tribunal meets in this building in San José. The members of the tribunal organize and supervise elections to ensure that they are fair and free.

elections and works to ensure that the electoral process is conducted fairly and legally. There are no jury trials in Costa Rica. Instead, judges decide all cases. Sometimes a case is handled by a single judge, and other times by a panel of judges.

The 1949 constitution does not allow the president, vice presidents, cabinet members, and Supreme Court judges to be Catholic clergy. Catholic religious leaders may serve in other political offices, however. The prohibition against serving in these high-level public offices does not apply to non-Catholic clergy.

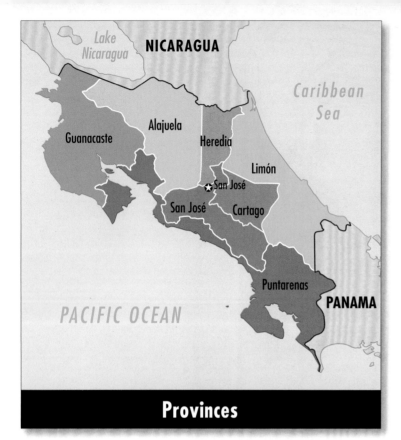

Provinces

Local Government

Costa Rica is divided into seven provinces. A governor appointed by the president manages each province. Provinces are divided into cantons, which are governed by a council elected by the voters. The people also elect municipal mayors. Cantons are further divided into districts. Currently there are eighty-one cantons and 473 districts in Costa Rica.

Law and Order

The constitution of 1949 disbanded Costa Rica's army and replaced it with the Civil Guard, which is responsible for maintaining law and order. The Civil Guard combines the functions of an army, navy, air force, police force, and coast guard.

Costa Rica's crime rate is relatively low. But in larger cities, especially San José, petty crimes, theft, and home invasions are on the rise. Illegal drugs are also a problem. In 2011, the Civil Guard consisted of about 4,500 officers. Costa Rica also has a border security police force, with about two thousand members. Local police forces throughout the provinces number about ten thousand strong.

Costa Rica's National Anthem

Costa Rica's national anthem is called "Noble patria, tu hermosa bandera" ("Noble Homeland, Your Beautiful Flag"). José María Zeledón wrote the words, and Manuel María Gutiérrez composed the music. The song became Costa Rica's official national anthem in 1949.

Spanish lyrics

Noble patria tu hermosa bandera,
expresión de tu vida nos da:
bajo el límpido azul de tu cielo,
blanca y pura descansa la paz.
En la lucha tenaz de fecund labor
queue enrojece del hombre la faz,
conquistaron tus hijos, labriegos sencillos,
eterno prestigio, estima y honor.

¡Salve, oh tierra gentil!
¡Salve, oh madre de amor!
Cando alguno pretenda tu gloria manchar,
verás a tu pueblo valiente y viril,
la tosca herramienta en arma trocar.
¡Salve patria! tu pródigo suelo
dulce abrigo y sustento nos da.
Bajo el límpido azul de tu cielo
¡Vivan siempre el trabajo y la paz!

English translation

Noble country, our lives
Are revealed in your flying flag;
For in peace, white and pure, we live tranquil
Beneath the clear limpid blue of your sky.
And their faces are ruddy with hard work
In the fields beneath the life-giving sun.
Though your sons are but farm workers, their labors eternal
Esteem, renown, and honor have won.

Hail, oh land of our birth!
Hail, oh gracious land we love!
If an enemy seeking to slander you or
Harm your name, then we will abandon our farms
And arise with fervor to take up our arms.
Oh, dear country, our refuge and shelter;
How fertile your life-giving soil!
May your people contented and peaceful
Unmolested continue their hard work.

CHAPTER 6

A Diverse Economy

A GRICULTURAL EXPORTS HAVE LONG PROVIDED THE foundation of Costa Rica's economy, but today industry and tourism are playing a greater role. Compared to other Central American countries, Costa Ricans enjoy a high standard of living. The gross domestic product (GDP), the total value of all goods and services produced in a country, per person in Costa Rica is $12,600. Roughly 25 percent of the nation lives in poverty. This is the lowest percentage among Central American countries.

Agriculture

About 10 percent of Costa Rica's land is devoted to agriculture. In 2012, agriculture accounted for an estimated 6.2 percent of the GDP and employed 14 percent of the workforce.

Bananas have been Costa Rica's leading export since the early twentieth century. Over the years, the industry has been hard-hit by banana diseases, workers' strikes, falling prices,

Opposite: **A worker carries a large bunch of bananas at a Dole company plantation in the Caribbean Lowlands. Hundreds of types of bananas exist around the world, but most grown for export are a variety called dwarf Cavendish. They have small seeds and are durable enough to withstand shipping.**

What Costa Rica Grows, Makes, and Mines

AGRICULTURE (2010)

Sugarcane	3,734,730 metric tons
Pineapples	1,976,760 metric tons
Bananas	1,803,940 metric tons

MANUFACTURING (VALUE ADDED)

Food products	US$734,000,000
Paints, soaps, and medicines	US$169,000,000
Plastic products	US$121,000,000

MINING

Limestone (2010)	1,500,000 metric tons
Gold (2009)	150 kilograms

and overproduction. Still, Costa Rica remains one of the world's largest exporters of bananas, second only to Ecuador. The banana industry employs about forty thousand workers. Another ten thousand people work indirectly in transportation, sales, and supplies. Most of the growing occurs on vast plantations located on the Caribbean plains and the Gulf of Dulce on the Pacific coast.

Costa Rica's first important export crop was coffee. The country is still known for its high-quality beans, and ranks thirteenth among world producers. The Central Valley provides ideal growing conditions for coffee production. Its fertile soil, high altitudes, and wet climate with a distinct dry season produce some of the world's finest beans.

In recent years, pineapple and sugarcane production have accounted for higher export earnings than coffee. Other important crops include cut flowers and tropical fruits, such as papayas, mangoes, and guavas. Melons, tomatoes, and avocados are also grown. Another major export is cacao, the beans from the cacao tree, which are used to make cocoa and chocolate. It is grown on small farms along the Caribbean coast and the southern and central Pacific coast.

About 70 percent of agricultural land in Costa Rica is devoted to cattle grazing. Guanacaste is the most important cattle region. About three-quarters of Costa Rica's 2.2 million cattle are raised there. Other livestock operations raise pigs, sheep, poultry, and goats.

Despite its extensive coastlines, Costa Rica's fishing industry is small. Large portions of the Caribbean coast have been des-

A cowboy herds cattle in the Guanacaste region. Cattle ranching used to be the main economic activity in Guanacaste, but tourism has grown in importance in recent years.

Costa Rican workers sew baseballs by hand. Every baseball used in Major League Baseball in the United States is made in Costa Rica.

ignated as national parks and are unavailable for fishing. About 90 percent of the annual fish harvest is caught in the Pacific Ocean. Small fishing operations catch tuna, herring, and sardines. Much of the fish is eaten locally or canned and shipped to the United States. Fish farms produce tilapia and shrimp.

Each year, thousands of sharks are killed off the coast of Costa Rica for their fins, which are considered a delicacy in China and elsewhere in East Asia. The practice is illegal but growing, and the Costa Rican government has had little success combating the problem.

Industry

In 2012, industry accounted for an estimated 21 percent of Costa Rica's GDP and employed about 22 percent of all workers. Costa Rica produces furniture, tobacco products, chemicals, plastic goods, and canned foods. Manufacturing textile and leather products are also big businesses. In the 1990s, several foreign-owned high-tech companies began operations in Costa Rica. Attracted by tax benefits, many of them manufacture computer chips and telecommunications equipment. Today, exports of electronics make up a significant portion of the country's GDP.

Costa Rica is one of the major manufacturers of baseballs used in the United States. A plant in Turrialba makes about 2.4 million balls a year and ships them to Miami, Florida. From there they are sold to buyers across the United States. Each ball is handmade. Interestingly, baseball is rarely played in Costa Rica.

Mining, Forestry, and Energy

Costa Rica has limited mineral resources. The production of minerals accounts for about only 1 percent of the GDP. Clay, sandstone, and limestone are among the leading products. Gold, silver, mercury, and salt are mined in small quantities.

Since the late 1940s, about 80 percent of Costa Rica's forests have disappeared. About 18 percent of the remaining forests are lightly used for lumber. Government regulations aimed at protecting the forests have resulted in a decline in lumber exports in recent years. About two-thirds of all the cut wood is used for fuel by Costa Ricans.

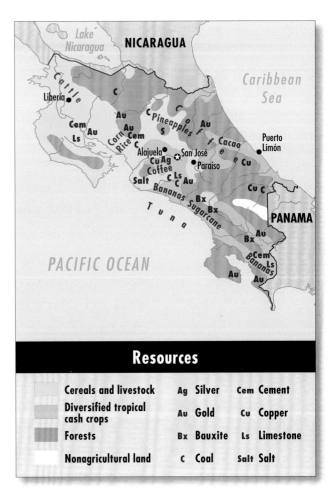

Resources

Cereals and livestock	Ag Silver	Cem Cement
Diversified tropical cash crops	Au Gold	Cu Copper
Forests	Bx Bauxite	Ls Limestone
Nonagricultural land	C Coal	Salt Salt

Costa Rica's unit of currency is the Costa Rican *colón*. One colón is divided into 100 *centimos*. Coins come in denominations of 5, 10, 25, 100, and 500 centimos. Paper money, or banknotes, is issued in denominations of 1,000, 2,000, 5,000, 10,000, 20,000, and 50,000 colones. In 2013, 500 Costa Rican colones equaled US$1.00.

The front of each banknote features an illustration of an important historical figure who contributed to Costa Rican democracy. The reverse side depicts a Costa Rican ecosystem and plant and animal species living within it. Each denomination is a different color. The yellow-tinted 5,000-colones banknote features Alfredo González Flores, who served as president from 1914 to 1917. An illustration of the Banco Internacional building appears in the background. The reverse side is illustrated with a mangrove ecosystem, featuring a white-faced capuchin, a mangrove tree, and a ghost crab.

The reddish-colored 20,000-colones note features María Isabel Carvajal, a noted writer and teacher, and an illustration from her book *Tales of My Aunt Panchita*. The reverse side shows a mountain ecosystem with a volcano hummingbird and the leaves of a native tree.

In its efforts to conserve its natural environment, Costa Rica gets about 99 percent of its electrical energy from clean sources. These include geothermal energy (from underground steam in volcanic regions), the burning of plant waste, and wind and solar energy. Hydroelectric dams provide the country's largest source of energy. They account for more than 82 percent of Costa Rica's electricity.

Services

Service industries, such as sales and tourism, employ about 64 percent of Costa Ricans and account for 73 percent of the nation's GDP. Many large banks and insurance companies are based in San José. Shopping malls and fast-food restaurants are commonplace in larger cities.

Today, many U.S. companies have some of their work done by businesses or individuals in Costa Rica. This allows the companies to reduce expenses because it costs less to hire workers in Costa Rica than in the United States. Hiring workers overseas to cut costs is called outsourcing. Costa Rica's political stability, high level of workers' education, and relatively close distance to the United States make it an ideal choice for U.S. companies. Much of the outsourced work comes from electronics and telecommunications businesses.

A worker checks computer parts at an Intel Corporation factory in San José. The American computer chip company employs 2,800 people in Costa Rica.

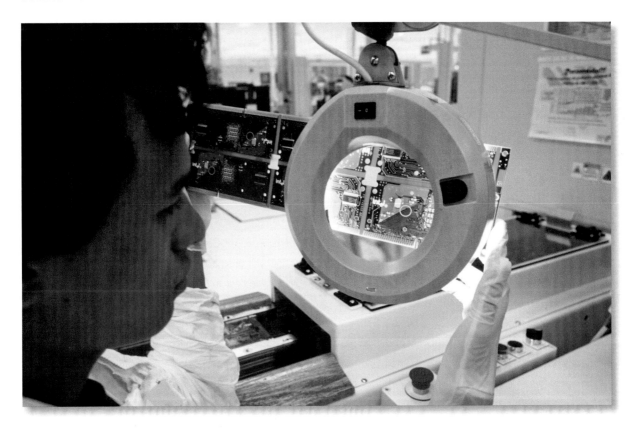

Since the late 1980s, tourism has exploded to become one of Costa Rica's most important industries. In 2010, tourism accounted for 5.5 percent of the GDP. In 2011, about 2.2 million visitors came to Costa Rica, bringing about $2.1 billion to the nation's economy. Most of the tourists come from the United States, Nicaragua, and Canada. Many visitors come to marvel at the beauty of Costa Rica's national parks and nature preserves. Among the favorites are the Arenal, Poás, and Irazú volcanoes and the Tortuguero, Santa Rosa, and Manuel Antonio national parks.

Foreign Trade

Throughout most of Costa Rica's history, agricultural products were its major exports. Today, however, computer microchips are its most valuable export. About 40 percent of the country's exports are shipped to the United States. Costa Rica's main regional trading partners are Mexico, Panama, and Guatemala. Roughly 25 percent of Costa Rica's exports

Medical Tourism

In 2011, an estimated forty thousand people visited Costa Rica to have medical or dental procedures done. Most were Americans or Canadians. This relatively new trend of traveling to foreign countries for care is called medical tourism. People do it to save money, because many procedures in Costa Rica cost only about 40 percent of what they cost in the United States and Canada. Even when adding in airfare and enough hotels and meals to enjoy Costa Rica's natural wonders, the cost is still less than having the procedure done at home. Many medical tourists come to Costa Rica for dental work. Medical tourism contributed $196 million to Costa Rica's economy in 2011. Medical tourists spent an additional $84 million on hotels, meals, travel, and shopping. The industry is rapidly growing and is becoming a vital part of Costa Rican tourism.

go to European nations such as the Netherlands, Germany, and England. Costa Rica also exports significantly to China and Hong Kong. The major exports are electronics, bananas, medical and surgical equipment, and coffee.

About 52 percent of Costa Rica's imports come from the United States. China, Mexico, Colombia, Brazil, and Guatemala are other major suppliers. Costa Rica imports parts used to build computers, medical equipment, and office machines, as well as materials for construction and heavy equipment. Oil and automobiles are also principal imports.

Costa Rica has trade agreements with several of its major trading partners, including the United States, Mexico, Canada, and China. The agreements allow Costa Rica to sell many of its products without paying taxes.

Coffee is roasted at a mill near San José. Coffee is one of Costa Rica's major export crops.

A public bus rumbles over a rough and wet road in the Caribbean Lowlands.

Transportation and Communication

Improved transportation and communication over the last few decades keep Costa Ricans linked to each other and to the world. The country has about 23,600 miles (38,000 km) of roadways, but only about 6,000 miles (9,600 km) are paved. The best roads are in the Central Valley, which serves as the main hub of the transportation network. From there, roadways extend to the Caribbean and Pacific coasts. Mountain roads are often washed out by heavy rains or destroyed by earthquakes, making travel through these areas hazardous. The Pan-American Highway, which runs from Alaska to the tip of South America, extends the length of the country, from the Nicaraguan border to Panama.

The main airport is the Juan Santamaría International Airport, located just outside San José. From there, passengers can hop direct flights to parts of North America, South America, and Europe. Three other airports also serve international destinations, while dozens of smaller airports offer local and regional service to all parts of the country.

Along its Caribbean coast, Costa Rica has two major ports, Limón and Moín. Caldera, located on the Gulf of Nicoya, is the main Pacific port. These ports are equipped to handle Costa Rica's export and import trade. Nearby, the port at Puntarenas handles only cruise ships.

Bus lines are one of the best ways to travel in Costa Rica. San José is the hub of bus transportation, although there is no central terminal. Large and small ticket offices are scattered throughout the city. Puerto Limón, Golfito, Puntarenas, and San Isidro also have large bus routes that connect urban and suburban areas. Car-and-passenger ferries and passenger-only ferries run from the Nicoya and Osa peninsulas to the mainland.

A Free Press

Costa Ricans have enjoyed freedom of the press since the nineteenth century. The nation's oldest and largest daily newspaper is *La Nacíon*, which was founded in 1946. *Diario Extra*, founded in the late 1970s, is well known for its use of bright red ink in its headlines. Each paper has a circulation of more than one hundred thousand. Other important dailies include *La República* and *La Prensa Libre*, the oldest newspaper in the country, founded in 1889. The *Tico Times* is published weekly in English. The staff of the newspaper is made up mostly of Americans who live in Costa Rica.

CHAPTER 7

Tico
Traditions

COSTA RICANS CALL THEMSELVES "TICOS," OR "Ticas" for females. The term probably comes from a colonial saying, "We are all *hermanticos*." In the Spanish language, the word *hermanticos* means "little brothers."

In recent decades, Costa Ricans have been moving from rural to urban areas in ever-increasing numbers. Cities and towns offer better health care, schools, and work opportunities. Today, about 60 percent of the population lives in cities. The rest lives in the countryside and remote rural regions. More than half of all Costa Ricans live in the Central Valley. Few people live on the northern Caribbean coast or on the southern Pacific coast and Nicoya Peninsula.

Costa Rica's population in 2013 was slightly less than 4.7 million people. It is a young nation, with 42 percent of the people under the age of twenty-four. Population growth has slowed dramatically in recent decades. In the 1960s, Costa Rican women had an average of seven children. Today, they have an average of two.

Population of Major Cities (2012 est.)

City	Population
San José	335,000
Puerto Limón	63,080
Alajuela	47,494
Liberia	45,380
Paraíso	39,700

A German restaurant in Nuevo Arenal. Costa Rica's magnificent environment has attracted many German immigrants in recent years.

European and Mestizo Costa Ricans

About 94 percent of all Ticos are of either European or mestizo background. Mestizos are people with mixed European and indigenous heritages.

Most Europeans came from Spain, but others arrived from Germany, Great Britain, and France. Many settled in the highlands and the Central Valley, where they dominated the coffee export industry. Today many landowning farming families are direct descendants of German immigrants who arrived in the mid-nineteenth century.

Black Costa Ricans

People of African descent are the largest minority group in Costa Rica, making up about 3 percent of the total population. Black immigrants began arriving in Costa Rica in 1824. Most black Costa Ricans are descendants of the West Indians, mainly from Jamaica, who came to build the railroad in the late nineteenth century. Most West Indians planned to return to Jamaica with their earnings, but many stayed on to work the banana plantations in the Caribbean Lowlands.

For many decades, many Ticos did not consider black people true Costa Ricans. Blacks from the West Indies spoke English and were subjects of the British government. They were not Catholic, like most other Costa Ricans, and they had established their own churches and schools. Because of these differences, black Costa Ricans traditionally lived apart from white Costa Ricans.

In the 1920s work in the highlands became difficult to find. Many Ticos moved to the Caribbean Lowlands to find work. This caused friction between the Ticos and the English-speaking blacks who were already working there. In the 1930s, disease devastated the United Fruit Company's banana operations in the Caribbean Lowlands. The company moved part of its operations to the Pacific coast, but Costa Rican laws did not allow the blacks to go along. Because blacks were denied citizenship, they did not have protection from this discrimination.

The status of blacks in Costa Rica changed dramatically in the late 1940s after President Figueres took office. Blacks had supported Figueres's cause and fought in the revolution. In 1948, Figueres declared that anyone born in Costa Rica had all the

Who Lives in Costa Rica? (2009 est.)	
Whites and mestizos	94%
Blacks	3%
Indigenous peoples	1%
Chinese	1%
Other	1%

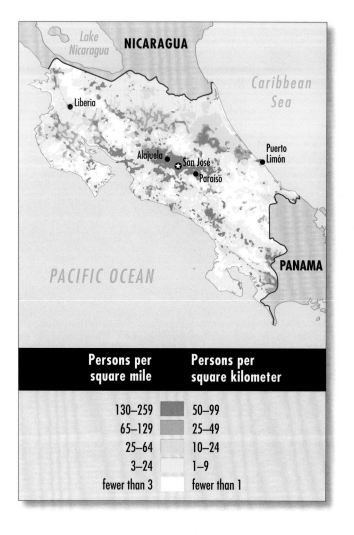

Persons per square mile	Persons per square kilometer
130–259	50–99
65–129	25–49
25–64	10–24
3–24	1–9
fewer than 3	fewer than 1

rights of citizenship. Black Costa Ricans now had equal rights, though this did not end everyday discrimination.

In the late 1950s, well-educated blacks began to work in professions. In the 1990s, Maureen Clarke was named minister of the interior, making her the country's first black cabinet member. Today, Puerto Limón is the center of the black population in Costa Rica, with people of African descent making up about 29 percent of the city's population.

Girls dressed for a parade in Puerto Limón

Indigenous Peoples

When Europeans began settling the region in the early six-teenth century, about four hundred thousand indigenous people lived in Costa Rica. As disease and warfare took their toll, however, the population declined drastically. Today, indigenous people make up about 1 percent of Costa Rica's total population. The largest indigenous groups today are the Bribrí, Cabécar, Guaymí, Boruca, and Maléku.

The Bribrí and Cabécar peoples live mainly on indigenous reserves, or reservations, in the Talamanca Range. They grow coffee, cacao, bananas, corn, and beans. Both groups retain their original language and still practice many of their ancient customs. Bribrí shamans, or religious healers, sing or chant to their gods to cure illness and disease.

The Guaymí people live mainly in the southern Pacific region along the Panama border. Guaymí farmers grow rice, beans, cacao, corn, and bananas. They hunt, fish, and raise

Bribrí children playing in a river. At least twelve thousand Bribrí people live in southern Costa Rica.

pigs. The Guaymí people are known for their colorful, hand-crafted traditional clothing and beaded necklaces, called *chaquiras*. They also produce garments, mats, and hats from tree bark. They often decorate these items with religious symbols and pictures of animals and plants.

The Boruca people, also known as the Brunca, live in several reservations in the province of Puntarenas. They plant crops and raise livestock. Borucas are known for their carved balsa wood masks painted to represent animal spirits. The masks are worn on the Fiesta de los Diablitos (Festival of Little Devils), a three-day celebration that takes place each December 30 to January 2. The festival celebrates the Borucas' victory over Spanish soldiers in the sixteenth century. During the festival, men dress in costumes and act out fights between Borucas and Spaniards.

The Maléku people live in the northern plains, mainly in Alajuela province. They speak both the Maléku language and Spanish. School lessons are provided in both languages in order to keep the traditional Maléku language alive. Malékus farm and grow pejibaye palm trees, which produce a highly nutritious, purple fruit. Skilled Maléku craftspeople create handsome figurines and ceramic items.

Since the arrival of Spaniards in Central America, the rights and welfare of Costa Rica's indigenous peoples have largely been ignored. It was not until 1956 that the government started to recognize the right of the indigenous peoples to preserve their land, and set up reserves. Nonindigenous people were banned from settling or developing the land. In

1973, the government established the National Commission for Indigenous Affairs (CONAI), with the purpose of improving the health, education, and economy of indigenous peoples.

Unfortunately, these measures failed to have a meaningful impact. Nonindigenous people invaded reserves and seized land to raise livestock, farm, and mine for minerals. CONAI was hit hard by economic woes in the 1970s and 1980s. It often lacked the funds to support and maintain its programs. Today, Costa Rica's indigenous people remain the poorest in the country.

Boruca people wear elaborate costumes during the Festival of Little Devils.

Chinese Costa Ricans carry a giant dragon puppet in a parade in San José.

In the 1990s, indigenous people began to demand a more prominent role in society. In 1992, they won the right to have school instruction in both Spanish and indigenous languages. They also gained political control over the country's twenty-four indigenous reserves. Finally, in 1994, they were granted full citizenship and the right to vote.

Chinese Costa Ricans

In 1855, a group of seventy-seven Chinese immigrants came to Costa Rica to help build railroads. In the early 1860s, laws were passed to prohibit further immigration from Asia. After the ban was lifted, in 1873, about six hundred Chinese immigrants came to Costa Rica. Many Chinese became household servants or merchants in San José and other large cities.

Costa Ricans of Chinese heritage are known as *chinos*. They make up about 1 percent of the country's total population. Many own shops, restaurants, and hotels in small towns in the lowlands. Some work as traders in the banana and cacao industries.

Recent Immigration

During the twentieth century, Germans, British, French, Italians, and South and North Americans settled in Costa Rica. Many of these people were attracted by Costa Rica's political and economic stability. The country's business regulations have attracted businesspeople who want to establish branches of their own foreign-owned companies. Many Americans have moved to Costa Rica to retire because they find the country friendly, peaceful, and beautiful.

Illegal Immigration

In recent years, illegal immigration has grown in Costa Rica. Nine percent of the people in Costa Rica were born in other countries. Many of those immigrants came from Nicaragua, where work is difficult to find. Once in Costa Rica, many work in construction, housekeeping, or as security guards. Thousands work on banana and coffee plantations during the harvest season.

The Costa Rican government has responded to the flow of immigrants by improving its border patrol. In the northern town of Peña Blanca, on the Nicaraguan border, Costa Rican authorities have built an 8-foot-high (2.4 m) wall to discourage migrants. Some Costa Ricans are sympathetic to the immigrants. A Costa Rican federal police officer said, "You can't help but feel sorry for them. Hunger doesn't need a passport."

Language

Spanish is the official language of Costa Rica. It is spoken by nearly everyone in the country. English is the second most common language and is now taught in all public schools. Some indigenous groups, such as the Bribrí and Maléku peoples, still speak their native languages. A few indigenous communities have established local radio broadcasts and newspapers that feature indigenous-language programs and news coverage.

Tico Spanish

Costa Ricans speak their own unique version of Spanish. They soften and slur the letter *r*, which makes the *r* sound nearly whistled. Latin Americans sometimes add the suffix *-ito*

Because tourism is a major industry in Costa Rica, many signs feature both Spanish and English.

Common Spanish Words and Phrases

sí	yes
no	no
buenos días	good morning
buenas noches	good night
¿Qué pasó?	What's up?
por favor	please
¿Habla inglés?	Do you speak English?
Me llamo . . .	My name is . . .
muchas gracias	thank you very much
adiós	good-bye

(EE-toh) or *-tito* (TEE-toh) to words. Instead of saying *momento* (moh-MEHN-toh), meaning "a moment," they will say *momentito* (moh-mehn-TEE-toh), which means a bit shorter than a moment. Costa Ricans instead use the forms *-ico* (EE-coh) or *-tico* (TEE-coh), so they say *momentico* (moh-mehn-TEE-coh). While Latin Americans transform *chico* (CHEE-koh), or "small," to *chiquito* (chee-KEE-toh), or "very little," Costa Ricans say *chiquitico* (chee-kee-TEE-koh), meaning "little bitty."

Costa Rican Spanish features *tiquismos* (tee-KEES-mohs), or expressions used only by Ticos. One tiquismo is *¡pura vida!* (POO-rah VEE-dah), which literally means "pure life." It is often used to mean "great!" or "terrific!" in answer to the question "How's it going?"

Costa Ricans like to call each other affectionate nicknames. A Tico might call his friend *flaco* (FLAH-koh), meaning "skinny," or *gordo* (GOR-doh), meaning "fat," no matter which the person is. Teenagers might call each other *maje* (MAH-hay), which means "sucker" or "dummy," but they use it to mean "pal" or "good buddy."

CHAPTER 8

A Tolerant Nation

T HE 1949 CONSTITUTION ESTABLISHED ROMAN Catholicism as Costa Rica's official religion. Yet the constitution also guarantees Costa Ricans the freedom to practice any religion they choose. Since the time the Spanish first arrived in the region, Catholicism has played an important role in Costa Rica's history. The missionaries built churches and missions where they taught the religion and converted indigenous people to Catholicism.

Catholicism Today

About 76 percent of Ticos consider themselves Roman Catholic, but less than half attend church regularly. The church, however, still serves an important social function in the heart of most communities. Nearly every town and suburb features a centrally located square with a church or cathedral. People frequently attend church for special occasions such as weddings, funerals, and baptisms. If a child is born Catholic, he or she is baptized as an infant. Many children are also given the rite of First Communion at age eight or nine.

Religions of Costa Rica

Roman Catholic	76%
Evangelical Protestant	14%
Jehovah's Witness	1%
Other and none	9%

Protestantism

Protestantism is the second most common religion in Costa Rica. About 14 percent of the population considers themselves Protestant. Protestantism was first established on the Caribbean coast. There, many black Costa Ricans, who traced their ancestry to Jamaica, belonged to the Baptist church. Baptist is a branch of Protestantism.

Beginning in the mid-1800s, North American Protestant missionaries began providing translations of the Bible to indigenous peoples in Costa Rica. Today, Protestant-based religious programs broadcast in Spanish from the United States reach hundreds of thousands of Costa Rican believers.

Protestant Costa Ricans include Methodists, Baptists, Episcopalians, Lutherans, and Jehovah's Witnesses. The Church of Jesus Christ of Latter-day Saints, whose followers are called Mormons, has about thirty-five thousand members nationwide.

The Mormon temple in San José is a regional center of worship serving Costa Rica, Nicaragua, Panama, and Honduras.

Other Religions

Non-Christian religions with followers in Costa Rica include Islam, Baha'i, and Judaism. An estimated four thousand Muslims, or followers of Islam, live in Costa Rica. The Baha'i faith came to Costa Rica in 1940, with the arrival of a Baha'i settler from the United States. An estimated 13,500 Baha'is now live in Costa Rica, mainly in the Central Valley. The first Jews arrived in Costa Rica in the sixteenth century to flee religious persecution in Spain. The present Jewish community arrived from Europe in the late 1920s. Most came from two small villages in Poland. Today, there are an estimated two thousand Jews in Costa Rica. Luis Liberman Ginsburg, a Costa Rican Jew whose family came from Poland, was elected one of Costa Rica's vice presidents in 2010.

Ancient Stories of Costa Rica

The ancient peoples who lived in fear of Costa Rica's frequent earth rumblings told stories to explain earthquakes and volcanoes. The Nahua people of Guanacaste believed that Central America lay on the back of a large but gentle caiman, a type of crocodile, called Cipactli. The creature was caught by Central American gods and turned on its back so it wouldn't escape. Now, whenever Cipactli twists and shakes to try to escape, the earth shakes with him.

The origin story of Irazú Volcano tells about a power-ful leader named Aquitaba and his daughter Irazú. His village was at war with a nearby village that wanted to control the region. Aquitaba took Irazú to the tallest mountaintop and offered her as a sacrifice to the gods to protect his village. The gods took Irazú. As the battle between the villages raged on, Aquitaba called on the spirit of his daughter to bring him victory. Instantly, the mountain began to belch fire and toss out rocks and ash, destroying the enemy and saving Aquitaba's people. From that day on, the mountain was called Irazú.

Indigenous Religions

Indigenous groups have kept many rituals and traditions of their ancient religious faiths. Sacred sites and animals are often believed to possess magical or supernatural powers. Many people believe that certain people have good or evil powers. In some indigenous communities, shamans are believed to heal the sick with prayers and music. Shamans often supervise events such as births and deaths among the Bribrí and Cabécar peoples.

Religious Celebrations

Many towns in Costa Rica are named after saints, people considered especially holy by the Catholic Church. Many cities, including the capital, San José, are named after Saint Joseph. On St. Joseph's Day, March 19, people attend street fairs and parades, often dressed in traditional clothing of red, white, and blue. Some attend special masses or observe the old tradition of visiting Poás Volcano.

Holy Thursday and Good Friday are celebrated in the week before Easter, called Holy Week. During that week, people participate in religious activities, including colorful processions held throughout the country. The processions often reenact events leading up to the death of Christ. The two days are national holidays. Most businesses and schools are closed. Many people use this time to go to the beach.

The largest celebration in Costa Rica is held each August 2 to celebrate the Feast of Our Lady of the Angels at the huge basilica in Cartago, near San José. More than two million

Basilica of Our Lady of the Angels

The Basilica of Our Lady of the Angels, located in Cartago, is one of Costa Rica's most important historical sites. This Roman Catholic church was built in 1639 and was almost totally destroyed in the 1910 earthquake near San José. The church that stands today was built in 1926 to look like the original.

Legend claims that a young peasant girl found a small, dark-colored statue on a rock in Cartago in 1635. The 3-inch-high (8 cm) statue depicted the Virgin Mary, Jesus's mother, holding the baby Jesus. The girl brought the statue home, but the next morning it was gone. She returned to the rock and discovered the statue sitting there. She took the statue to her local priest, and he locked it up for the night. The next morning, the statue was no longer locked up. Instead, it was back on the rock. At the time, the basilica was being built in another location. After earthquakes interrupted construction, officials decided to move construction and build the church on the spot where the girl found the statue.

The original statue is kept in the church. It is affectionately called La Negrita, or the Black Virgin, because of its dark color. Each August about 2.5 million worshippers come to the Basilica of Our Lady of the Angels to celebrate the appearance of the Black Virgin, Costa Rica's patron saint, and pray before La Negrita.

people from around the country and the world journey to the Basilica of Our Lady of the Angels to celebrate a miracle that is said to have taken place in 1635 involving a tiny statue of Mary, the mother of Jesus. Many of the pilgrims walk the 10 miles (16 km) from San José, some entering the basilica on

Priests celebrating the Feast of Our Lady of the Angels hold up a tiny statue said to have performed miracles.

their hands and knees as a sign of religious devotion. A procession travels from the basilica to the nearby Church of St. Nicholas. The route of the procession is decorated with carpets of flowers and colored sand.

Christmas

Christmas celebrations in Costa Rica begin many days in advance of December 25. In the middle of December, El Carnaval brings together dancers and musical groups from across the country to compete in talent events. A parade called El Tope features show horses, beautiful horse-drawn carriages, and hand-painted oxcarts. In San José, the grand El Tope parade also features floats, clowns, and marching bands. The event is broadcast on television throughout the country. El Desfile de Luces (The Parade of Lights) is a nighttime event with marching bands, fireworks, and performers under thousands of bright Christmas lights.

A few days before Christmas, families put up their Christmas trees. The trees are often small, fragrant cypresses or branches from a coffee plant or evergreen tree. They are usually painted white and decorated with lights, small figurines, and colored strips of paper. A gold star is placed atop the tree.

On Christmas Eve, most families have a late dinner of pork and tamales, a traditional Central American dish of cornmeal dough stuffed with meat, cheese, or vegetables and wrapped in a banana or plantain leaf. Many Costa Ricans then go to midnight mass. On Christmas Day, children play with the presents they have received and families visit with one another. In some communities, families attend the Fiesta de Zapote, a fair that includes thrill rides and music. The main feature, though, is the bullring. Bulls with riders are let loose in the ring in a competition to see which rider can stay on the longest. Christmas celebrations in Costa Rica end on January 6.

Costumed dancers parade through the streets of San José during the Parade of Lights.

CHAPTER 9

Arts and Sports

COSTA RICA HAS PRODUCED MANY ACCOMPLISHED writers, artists, musicians, and performers. After the 1949 constitution was adopted, the government increased its support of the arts and began to fund the theater, music, and arts groups. In the 1950s, under President José Figueres Ferrer, the government founded the Castellan Conservatory, which has trained thousands of young Costa Rican musicians and dancers. At the end of the decade, the Costa Rican government established Editorial Costa Rica, a publishing house that promotes the work of Costa Rican writers.

During his second presidential term in the 1970s, Figueres added to his legacy by creating the Ministry of Culture, Youth, and Sports, and the Youth Symphony Orchestra. Both organizations are highly respected institutions and are symbols of the pride that Costa Ricans take in their country's lively culture.

Opposite: **A statue celebrating music stands outside the National Theater in San José.**

Art

Until the 1920s, Costa Rican art was largely influenced by European artists. Teodórico Quirós (1897–1977) and Fausto Pacheco (1899–1966) were the first Costa Rican painters to establish a style that represented true Costa Rican culture. The style, called *costumbrismo*, depicted scenes of Costa Rican customs and daily life. The art of *costumbristas*, the people who

Many of Francisco Zúñiga's works, such as this 16-inch-high (41 cm) bronze, show women sitting or squatting.

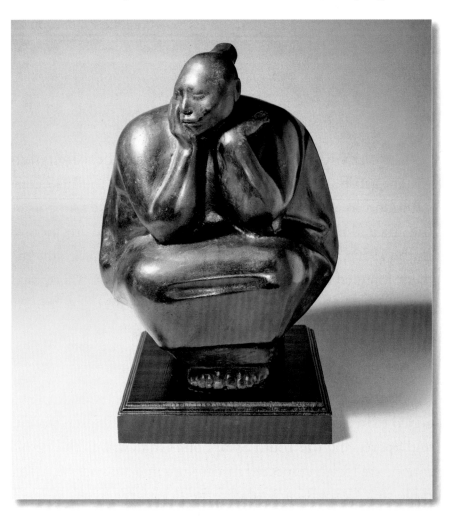

painted in this style, often featured the country's rolling hills and lush rain forests, with traditional adobe houses.

Francisco Zúñiga (1912–1998) and Francisco Amighetti (1907–1998) both depicted ordinary men and women in their art. Zúñiga, Costa Rica's best-known sculptor, was renowned for his bronze works depicting indigenous women. Amighetti was an engraver who also painted and wrote poetry. He introduced mural painting, or large paintings on walls, to Costa Rica.

Max Jiménez (1900–1947) studied art in Paris, France. After sculpting influential works in stone and bronze, he began oil painting. Rather than presenting idealized images of Costa Rica's natural beauty, he often depicted images of blacks and indigenous people of the Caribbean coast.

A more recent Costa Rican artist is Isidro Con Wong (1931–), who was born in Puntarenas to Chinese immigrant parents. He studied in Asia and returned to his home in Nicoya where he farmed, fished, and raised cattle. Working the land influenced his art, which often features landscapes, moons, and bulls. He frequently incorporates Chinese words and characters in the trees he draws, hiding them from the viewer.

María Isabel Carvajal appears on the twenty thousand colones bill. The bill also shows a rabbit petting a wolf, a scene from her book *Tales of My Aunt Panchita*.

Literature

Much of the work of Costa Rica's top writers addresses social problems. María Isabel Carvajal (1888–1949), who wrote under the name Carmen Lyra, was the first woman to be widely published in Costa Rica. Lyra often wrote about her country's social and economic injustices, but she also wrote *Christmas Fantasy*, a popular children's play, and *Tales of My Aunt Panchita*.

Carlos Luis Fallas (1909–1966) exposed the abuses of the banana companies in *Mamita Yunai*, which first appeared as weekly installments in a local newspaper. The novel describes the poor working conditions of the United Fruit Company's black and indigenous workers. It also documents the company's destruction of the environment.

Many people consider Carmen Naranjo (1928–2012) Costa Rica's most influential author. Many of her novels, short stories, plays, and poetry focus on issues such as society and women's rights. *Diary of a Crowd* portrays the middle class as being detached from reality and blind to society's ills. In it, she tackles the impact of modernization on contemporary life. Naranjo served as Minister of Culture, Youth, and Sports and as an ambassador to Israel.

Dance

Dance in Costa Rica ranges from classical to folk to popular. In recent years, ballet has become extremely popular for young girls.

The National Dance Company, based in San José, has been training dancers since the 1980s. The most talented often represent Costa Rica in international cultural events. In recent years, the company has increasingly embraced modern dance in its repertoire.

Ballet dancers perform in San José.

Most traditional Costa Rican folk dances originated in the Guanacaste province. Many people consider *punto Guanacasteco* (Guanacaste dance step) the typical Costa Rican folk dance. The dance represents a courtship between a man and a woman. Couples stomp to music played on a guitar and a marimba, a type of xylophone. Occasionally, the dancers stop, and a male dancer shouts out a witty verse about how the dancers are performing. El Torito (the little bull) is a dance portraying the man as a bull and the woman as a bullfighter. The woman dances, seemingly unaware that the man is trying to kiss her. Eventually, she controls him with her cape, represented by a bandanna.

Punto Guanacasteco is a traditional dance that arose out of the rural culture of the Guanacaste region. Today, it is performed mostly at festivals and parades.

Throughout the country, Costa Ricans flock to local dance halls to dance to Latin rhythms, such as salsa and merengue. On the Caribbean coast, many people dance to reggae and calypso music.

The marimba is a popular instrument in Costa Rica. It consists of wooden bars of different lengths, each producing a different note. A marimba may be played by one person, or by more than one person at the same time.

Theater

San José is the center of theater in Costa Rica. The National Theater supports a wide range of plays and performances. The smaller Angel Theater features new works by modern Costa Rican writers as well as classical Greek and Roman plays. The theater also stages comedies, dances, and social satires. It was established in the 1970s by Chilean refugees fleeing Chile's military dictatorship. Their efforts helped revitalize Costa Rican theater and provide opportunities for countless Costa Rican performers.

The National Theater

Standing in the heart of San José is the National Theater. A symbol of Costa Rica's cultural pride, the theater hosts a wide variety of performances, including opera, ballet, concerts, and plays.

Construction on the theater began in 1891. Wealthy coffee growers wanted to have a place to house cultural events of all types. They placed taxes on each bag of coffee they produced to raise money to build the theater. Soon, artists, craftspeople, teachers, students, and merchants began making donations to complete the building. The National Theater finally opened in 1897.

The building was designed in a neoclassical style, which is based on Classical Greek and Roman architecture. Some people consider it San José's greatest historic building. Its lavish interiors feature marble statues. The inside ceiling is adorned with a mural called the *Allegory of Coffee and Bananas*, which pays tribute to the coffee growers who financed the theater's construction, and to bananas, Costa Rica's main agricultural product.

Early Costa Rican plays often focused on humor and rural characters, but by the late nineteenth century, the works had become darker. Ricardo Fernández Guardia (1867–1950) is considered by many people to be the father of Costa Rican theater. In *Magdalena*, he wrote about the urbanization of his country and how it threatened the Costa Rican way of life.

In the 1920s, playwrights such as Daniel Ureña (1876–1933) focused on the clash between traditional values and the rapidly modernizing world. By the 1960s and 1970s, political and moral issues became the focus of popular playwrights such as Alberto Cañas (1920–) and Daniel Gallegos (1930–). Their works often explored the meaning of life and the power of the common people. In recent years, Jorge Arroyo (1959–)

has emerged as one of Costa Rica's best-known playwrights. He often writes about historical figures, Costa Rican traditions, and the role of men and women in society. His plays have been staged throughout Latin America and have been translated into English and Portuguese.

Music

Traditional Costa Rican music dates back thousands of years, to the time when indigenous peoples made musical instruments by hand. Variations of those instruments are still played today. The *quijongo* was traditionally made with a single string of hemp fiber and a thin wooden neck. They were attached to

Guitars are common instruments in Costa Rican folk music.

a hollowed-out gourd, a squash-like, hard-skinned fruit. The string was plucked or played with a bow. Today the quijongo is made with a wooden box instead of a gourd. Early marimbas were made from a series of hollow gourds and wooden keys, which were hit with sticks to produce different tones.

Guanacaste province has produced many of Costa Rica's best-known composers, whose most popular works are romantic ballads. The instruments that accompany these gentle songs are guitars, a marimba, and a pair of maracas, which are hollowed out gourds filled with dried seeds. In Limón province, calypso and reggae brought from the Caribbean Islands are popular.

Today, Costa Ricans enjoy an unlimited choice of musical styles. Throughout the country, music lovers can hear classical, rock, jazz, folk, hip-hop, merengue, metal, and punk. Much of the popular music is blended with Latin styles, producing unique hybrids of musical forms.

Bringing Home Gold

Swimmer Claudia Poll Ahrens was the first Costa Rican athlete to win a gold medal in the Olympic Games. In 1996, she captured the gold in the 200-meter freestyle swim. Poll was born in Managua, Nicaragua, in 1972. She began swimming when she was seven years old. At 6 feet 3 inches (1.9 m) tall, Poll was one of the tallest women swimmers of her day. She continued her medal-winning ways in the 2000 Olympics, bringing home two bronze medals. Her older sister Sylvia was also a competitive swimmer. Sylvia won Costa Rica's first Olympic medal, capturing a silver in the 1988 Games.

Sports

Soccer is the favorite sport in Costa Rica. It is played year-round throughout the country, by children and adults, from small towns and villages to San José's thirty-five-thousand-seat National Stadium of Costa Rica. Costa Rica's national soccer team plays in the Costa Rican Football Federation, the country's national professional soccer league.

Costa Rica's mild climate and natural beauty attract outdoor sports lovers of all kinds. Surfers from around the world come to Costa Rica's Pacific coast to ride the crashing waves. Sea fishing is popular on both coasts. Mountain climbers can push themselves to the limit in the country's rugged mountains. Lake Arenal's strong and steady winds from November to April create ideal windsurfing conditions. Scuba diving, white-water rafting, and kayaking have also become major attractions for sports enthusiasts on the go.

Costa Ricans and tourists alike enjoy surfing and relaxing on Costa Rica's endless beaches.

CHAPTER 10

Daily Life

COSTA RICANS ARE PROUD OF THEIR COUNTRY AND appreciate its long history of peace, education, and democracy. Ticos identify strongly with being Costa Ricans, rather than considering themselves Central Americans. Costa Ricans tend to be cheerful and friendly to strangers.

Opposite: **A boy relaxes on the porch of a wooden house in Puerto Limón.**

Housing

The type of houses that Costa Ricans live in depends upon their wealth and where the houses are located. In cities in the Central Valley, working-class people live in houses made of concrete blocks or bricks. Most are one story and are painted in bright green, blue, or pink. The houses usually have a main room, a kitchen, a bathroom, and two or three bedrooms.

Wealthier people in the Central Valley often live in two-story houses with a porch and lawn in front. The houses are frequently surrounded by fences or gates, and may have iron grilles over the windows. Larger houses may also have garages and swimming pools.

Many poor people in cities live wherever they can find shelter. Their homes are frequently unpainted, broken-down shacks made of wood, corrugated steel, or cardboard. The floors may be dirt or wooden planks.

Homes in more remote areas of the Central Valley are usually built of adobe with a roof of clay tiles. Homes on the coastal lowlands are commonly built of wood. The homes are erected on stilts to protect the houses from flooding.

Houses in the Caribbean Lowlands are typically elevated to keep them safe from heavy rains and frequent flooding.

Health

Costa Rica has long been recognized for its high standard of health care. The country has been rated as having one of the twenty best health care systems in the world, and the best in Latin America. Today, the government provides free or low-cost health coverage to all citizens and permanent legal residents. In the 1970s, the government began programs providing health care in remote rural communities. It set up vaccination programs, welfare programs, and a social security system to assist the aged and sick. Along with doctor and nurse visits to these areas, the government's efforts helped reduce poverty and disease significantly.

In Costa Rica, men live an average of seventy-five years, and women an average of eighty-one years. These are the highest life expectancies in Central America. The country's infant death rate of 8.9 deaths per 1,000 births is by far the lowest in the region.

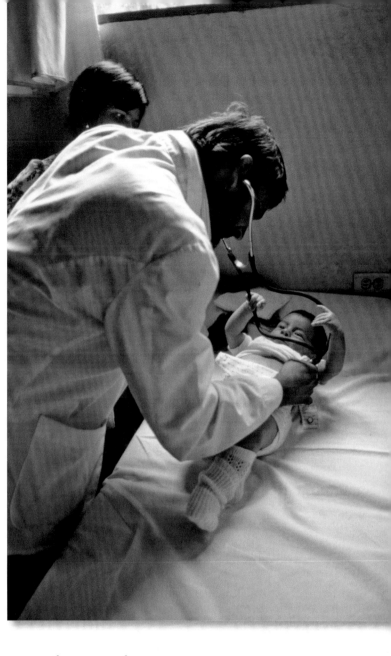

A doctor in a Costa Rican clinic gives a baby a checkup. Costa Rica has the lowest rate of infant death of any country in Central America.

Students gather around a teacher at a school along the Caribbean coast. Costa Rican schools have an average of about twenty-eight students per class.

Education

Since it became independent, Costa Rica has shown a steady commitment to education. Public education was established during the 1820s. In 1869, education became free and mandatory. During the 1940s and 1950s, the government increased its commitment to education. Teachers' salaries and pensions were increased and schools were opened in most remote rural areas.

Because Costa Rica does not have to support a military, it can instead spend money on many social and cultural needs, including education. Costa Rica currently spends about 6.3 percent of its gross national product on education. This is one of the highest rates in the region. Costa Rica's educational system is considered among the best in Latin America. Today, 96 percent of adult Costa Ricans can read and write.

In Costa Rica, the school year runs from February to October. Students attend primary school for nine years, the equivalent of first to ninth grades in the United States. After completing their early education, students may either go to work or attend high school. There they can choose from an academic program or a job-training program in health, business, art, or other vocations. To graduate, high school students must complete 30 hours of community service.

The government funds five public universities: University of Costa Rica in San Pedro, National Autonomous University in Heredia, Cartago's Institute of Technology, State Distance Education University, and Technical University in Alajuela. Students wishing to graduate from a public university must complete 150 hours of community service for a bachelor's degree, and

All Costa Rican students are required to wear uniforms through ninth grade.

National Holidays

New Year's Day	January 1
St. Joseph's Day	March 19
Holy Thursday	March or April
Good Friday	March or April
Juan Santamaría Day (Battle of Rivas)	April 11
Labor Day	May 1
Our Lady of the Angels	August 2
Feast of the Assumption/Mother's Day	August 15
Independence Day	September 15
All Souls' Day	November 2
Feast of the Immaculate Conception	December 8
Christmas Day	December 25

300 hours for a master's degree. In recent years, private colleges and universities have grown considerably. There are roughly eighty private universities spread throughout Costa Rica.

Food

Costa Rican food is a blend of indigenous foods and those introduced by the Spaniards. Potatoes, corn, fruits, and turkey are native to Costa Rica. The Europeans brought meats such as pork and beef. The most common ingredients used in Costa Rican cooking are rice, beans, corn, potatoes, and plantains, which are starchy bananas. Tortillas, thin flatbreads made from corn flour, can be topped with beans, beef, and cheese. Tamales filled with a variety of meats and vegetables and topped with chili sauce are popular. *Picadillo* is another traditional dish. It is made with beef, tomatoes, rice, and peppers.

A typical Costa Rican breakfast might include *gallo pinto*, a mixture of black beans and white rice, flavored with

onions, pepper, and other spices. It is often served with eggs. Lunchtime meals often feature *casado*, a dish made with rice, beans, eggs, and pasta. Dinner might be *olla de carne*, a Spanish stew made with beef, corn, squash, and other vegetables.

Ceviche is Costa Rica's most popular fish dish, often eaten as an appetizer. It is usually made with shrimp, shellfish, or sea bass that has been marinated in lemon or lime juice, onion, garlic, and cilantro.

Fruits are widely used in juices and desserts. Popular fruits include pineapples, mangoes, guavas, and papayas. Desserts include *dulce de ayote*, a sweet mixture of squash, sugar, cinnamon, cloves, and orange peel. *Empanadas de piña* are sweet, baked turnovers filled with pineapple jam. *Pan de yuca*, or yucca bread, is made with yucca starch, cheese, butter, and eggs. It is often sold in street markets and is best to eat when it is warm.

Bread or Cake?

Pan de elote, or sweet corn bread, is a favorite dessert among Costa Ricans. But don't let its name fool you: It's more of a luscious, pudding-like cake than a bread. Try this easy-to-make recipe with an adult's help.

Ingredients

2 cups corn kernels, ground or
    liquefied in a food processor

¾ cup buttermilk

4 eggs, whipped

1 cup brown sugar

2 cups all-purpose flour

3 teaspoons baking soda

½ teaspoon salt

$\frac{1}{8}$ teaspoon cinnamon

1 stick butter or margarine

Directions

Combine the corn, buttermilk, whipped eggs, and brown sugar in a bowl. Add the flour, baking soda, salt, cinnamon, and butter or margarine. Mix until smooth. Bake the mixture in a square cake pan at 350°F for 40 minutes. Let the bread cool for about 15 minutes, cut into squares, and serve. Enjoy!

The most popular drink in Costa Rica is coffee. People like to drink it strong and very sweet. Other popular beverages include *batido*, a fruit juice mixed with water or milk. *Horchata*, another sweet drink, is made from cornmeal and cinnamon. Costa Ricans' love of sweets is also demonstrated in the use of chocolate in many drinks and desserts. Chocolate

A man makes coffee at a restaurant in Costa Rica. On average, Costa Ricans drink nearly as much coffee as people in the United States do.

candies called *milanes* and chocolate-topped ice cream known as *cono capuchino* are much loved.

The food prepared on the Caribbean coast is spicier than that eaten in the highlands. Cumin, paprika, coriander, and chilis are some of the spices often used. Coconut milk and coconut oil are popular ingredients for many dishes, including coconut custard and braised shrimp. Rundown is a stew made

Ice cream is growing in popularity in Costa Rica.

A Day at the Market

Three types of markets serve the food-buying needs of most Costa Ricans:

Traditional outdoor markets are made up of rows of booths selling fruits and vegetables, cooked foods such as tamales, and even livestock such as chickens or pigs. Vendors also offer handmade items such as leather goods, clothing, toys, and baskets. The San José Central Market, the city's largest open-air market, features more than two hundred shops. They sell everything from food to saddles to musical instruments. The market has been around since 1880, and tens of thousands of people visit it daily.

A *pulpería*, or general store, is similar to an American grocery store, offering an assortment of processed and canned foods, food staples, and cleaning and household supplies.

In recent years, large, modern malls have sprung up in towns and cities throughout Costa Rica. Many Costa Ricans now shop in these malls, which feature well-stocked supermarkets, movie theaters, food courts, and brand-name boutiques.

with meat or fish and vegetables such as cassavas, potatoes, bananas, or plantains. Rice, beans, cabbage, corn, carrots, tomatoes, and peanuts are widely eaten, and are mainly imported from inland regions.

People who live along the coast eat more seafood than people living in other areas in Costa Rica. Lobster, squid, and conch are frequent treats for Caribbean and Pacific coast residents. For Ticos and for tourists who have come to enjoy all that Costa Rica has to offer, a delicious seafood soup is the perfect way to end a long day on the beach.

Timeline

People begin settling in what **ca. 12,000 BCE** is now Costa Rica.

People in Costa Rica begin trading **ca. 800 BCE** with the Maya to the north.

People in Costa Rica create **ca. 200 BCE-** large stone spheres. **1500 CE**

Christopher Columbus **1502** lands in Costa Rica.

Spaniard Gil González Dávila explores **1522** Costa Rica's Pacific coast.

Cartago, Costa Rica's first permanent **1563** European settlement, is founded.

An eruption of Irazú **1723** Volcano destroys Cartago.

San José is founded. **1737**

ca. 2500 BCE The Egyptians build the pyramids and the Sphinx in Giza.

ca. 563 BCE The Buddha is born in India.

313 CE The Roman emperor Constantine legalizes Christianity.

610 The Prophet Muhammad begins preaching a new religion called Islam.

1054 The Eastern (Orthodox) and Western (Roman Catholic) Churches break apart.

1095 The Crusades begin.

1215 King John seals the Magna Carta.

1300s The Renaissance begins in Italy.

1347 The plague sweeps through Europe.

1453 Ottoman Turks capture Constantinople, conquering the Byzantine Empire.

1492 Columbus arrives in North America.

1500s Reformers break away from the Catholic Church, and Protestantism is born.

1776 The U.S. Declaration of Independence is signed.

1789 The French Revolution begins.

COSTA RICAN HISTORY

1821 Costa Rica declares independence from Spain.

1823 Costa Rica joins the United Provinces of Central America.

1838 The United Provinces of Central America is dissolved, and Costa Rica becomes fully independent.

1843 The first shipment of Costa Rican coffee is sent to England.

1856 Costa Rican troops defeat the invasion by American William Walker.

1870 General Tomás Guardia overthrows the government of Costa Rica.

1870s The nation's first banana plantations are established.

1910 A railroad connecting San José to the Pacific coast is completed.

1940s President Rafael Ángel Calderón Guardia introduces social and labor reforms.

1948 Civil war erupts in Costa Rica; after the war, the army is dissolved.

1949 Costa Rica enacts a new constitution.

1950s President José Figueres Ferrer expands Costa Rica's education and health systems.

1987 President Óscar Arias Sánchez wins the Nobel Peace Prize for his attempts to bring peace to Central America.

2010 Laura Chinchilla becomes the first woman elected president of Costa Rica.

WORLD HISTORY

1865 The American Civil War ends.

1879 The first practical lightbulb is invented.

1914 World War I begins.

1917 The Bolshevik Revolution brings communism to Russia.

1929 A worldwide economic depression begins.

1939 World War II begins.

1945 World War II ends.

1969 Humans land on the Moon.

1975 The Vietnam War ends.

1989 The Berlin Wall is torn down as communism crumbles in Eastern Europe.

1991 The Soviet Union breaks into separate states.

2001 Terrorists attack the World Trade Center in New York City and the Pentagon near Washington, D.C.

2004 A tsunami in the Indian Ocean destroys coastlines in Africa, India, and Southeast Asia.

2008 The United States elects its first African American president.

Fast Facts

Official name:	Republic of Costa Rica
Capital:	San José
Official language:	Spanish

San José

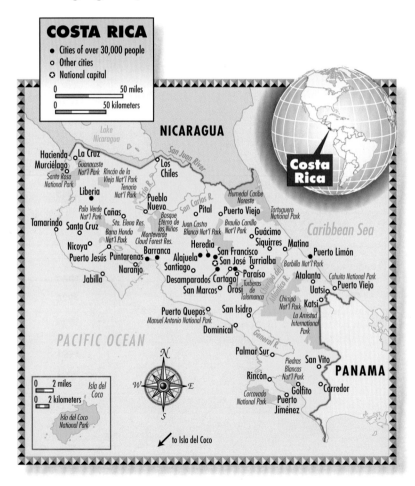

Costa Rican flag

Manuel Antonio National Park

Year of founding:	1848
Official religion:	None
National anthem:	"Noble patria, tu hermosa bandera" ("Noble Homeland, Your Beautiful Flag")
Government:	Democratic republic
Head of state:	President
Head of government:	President
Area of country:	19,730 square miles (51,100 sq km)
Latitude and longitude of geographic center:	10°0' N, 84°0' W
Bordering countries:	Nicaragua to the north, Panama to the southeast
Highest elevation:	Chirripó Grande, 12,530 feet (3,819 m) above sea level
Lowest elevation:	Sea level along the coasts
Average daily high temperature:	80°F (27°C) in San José; 86°F (30°C) in Puerto Limón
Average daily low temperature:	65°F (18°C) in San José; 71°F (22°C) in Puerto Limón
Average annual rainfall:	Caribbean Lowlands, 150 to 200 inches (380 to 500 cm); Central Valley and mountains, 70 inches (180 cm); Pacific coast, 130 inches (330 cm)

Monteverde Cloud Forest Reserve

National population (2013 est.):	4,695,942

Population of major cities (2012 est.):

San José	335,000
Puerto Limón	63,080
Alajuela	47,494
Liberia	45,380
Paraíso	39,700

Landmarks:
- ▶ *Arenal Volcano*, Alajuela
- ▶ *Basilica of Our Lady of the Angels*, Cartago
- ▶ *Guayabo National Monument*, Turrialba
- ▶ *Jade Museum*, San José
- ▶ *Monteverde Cloud Forest Reserve*, Santa Elena
- ▶ *National Theater*, San José

Economy: Costa Rica's traditional crops of bananas, sugar, coffee, and beef are mainstays of export trade. In recent years, specialized agricultural products such as pineapples, melons, beans, and potatoes have become more common. The manufacturing of computer chips, medical equipment, textiles and clothing, and construction materials is also important to the economy. Costa Rica's natural beauty attracts tourists from around the globe. Many foreign nations and businesses have invested in Costa Rica because it is politically stable and has a well-educated population.

Currency: The colón. In 2013, 500 colones equaled US$1.00.

System of weights and measures: Metric system

Literacy rate (2012): 96%

Currency

Students

José Figueres Ferrer

Common Spanish words and phrases:

sí	yes
no	no
buenos días	good morning
buenas noches	good night
¿Qué pasó?	What's up?
por favor	please
¿Habla inglés?	Do you speak English?
Me llamo . . .	My name is . . .
muchas gracias	thank you very much
adiós	good-bye

Prominent Costa Ricans:

Francisco Amighetti (1907–1998)
Artist

Óscar Arias Sánchez (1940–)
President and Nobel Peace Prize winner

Ibo Bonilla Oconitrillo (1951–)
Architect, sculptor, and educator

Laura Chinchilla (1959–)
President

José Figueres Ferrer (1906–1990)
President

Carmen Naranjo (1928–2012)
Writer and poet

Claudia Poll Ahrens (1972–)
Olympic gold medalist swimmer

Juan Santamaría (1831–1856)
National hero

To Find Out More

Books

▶ Foley, Erin, and Barbara Cooke. *Costa Rica*. New York: Marshall Cavendish, 2006.

▶ Forsyth, Adrian. *Nature of the Rainforest: Costa Rica and Beyond.* Ithaca, NY: Comstock, 2008.

▶ Shields, Charles J. *Costa Rica*. Philadelphia: Mason Crest, 2009.

DVDs

▶ *Families of Costa Rica*. Master Communication, Inc., 2008.

▶ *Living Landscapes: Costa Rica*. CustomFlix, 2006.

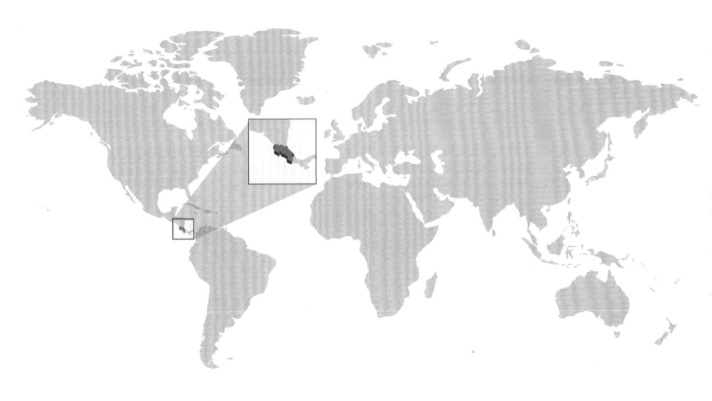

▶ Visit this Scholastic Web site for more information on Costa Rica:
www.factsfornow.scholastic.com
Enter the keywords Costa Rica

Index

Page numbers in *italics*
indicate illustrations.

Meet the Author

NEL YOMTOV IS AN AWARD-WINNING AUTHOR and editor with a passion for writing nonfiction books for young people. Bitten by the reading bug at an early age, he learned how books could be the doorway to the wonders of our world and its people. Writing gives him an opportunity to investigate the subjects he loves best and to share his discoveries with young readers. In recent years, he has written books about history and geography as well as graphic-novel adaptations of classic mythology, sports biographies, and science topics.

Yomtov was born in New York City. After graduating college, he worked at Marvel Comics, where he handled all phases of comic book production. By the time he left seven years later, he was supervisor of the product development division of Marvel's licensing program. Yomtov has also written, edited, and colored hundreds of Marvel comic books.

He has served as editorial director of a children's nonfiction book publisher and also as publisher of the Hammond World Atlas book division. In between, he squeezed in a two-year stint as consultant to Major League Baseball, where he helped supervise an educational program for elementary and middle schools throughout the country.

Yomtov lives in the New York area with his wife, Nancy, a teacher and writer, and son, Jess, a writer and radio broadcaster. He spends his leisure hours on the softball fields in New York City's Central Park and at neighborhood blues clubs playing harmonica with local bands.

Photo Credits